R F
OUR

Gary
You Are in my thoughts & Prayers Daily.

You Are a bigger part of my life than I am sure you know.

Love
Susan

 # <u>Reviews</u>

WOW! This is definitely one of the most inspirational books I have ever read. Small book...HUGE impact! It sits on my night stand to read over and over again. Kerry K., Artist

Wow! Very powerful risk-taking writing! Dr. P., Dean, Arts and Social Services (Re: Essay called "Collapsing and Rebirthing")

This could be a blueprint for world unity. Ron D., Carpenter

We enjoyed reading your beautiful booklet. Plant a seed and help it grow. Dr. Casey G., Doctor of Divinity

I loved it! Especially the poems—so beautiful! Saying a lot with so few words is a rare talent. Fran S., Corporate Office Manager

I'd read a line and want to think about it all day. It really warmed my heart! Patti S., Real Estate Entrepreneur

I finished reading your book, put it down and cried. I can't say why. It seemed to validate me in some way. Write more...Joanne L., Teacher

Your words are celestial music to my heart. I have re-read your words and each time my heart opens. Tears come; joy is within the tears. Susan C., Metaphysician

What you write is so true. Happiness is a choice. Faithe G., Social Worker

Oh my God! Unbelievable! It sits on my coffee table to share with everyone I love. Bonnie, O'H., Social Worker

Panorama Publishing Co.
Box 1127, Peachland, British Columbia
VOH 1XO, CANADA
Tel: 250.215.1831 E-Mail: randidone@hotmail.com
www.panorama-publishing.ca

ISBN: 978-0-9782691-0-4

Library and Archives Canada Cataloguing in Publication

Done, Randi, 1956-
    Reaching our greater destiny / Randi Done.

Includes bibliographical references.
ISBN 978-0-9782691-0-4

        1. Spiritual life. I. Title.

BL624.D64 2007   **204'.4**   **C2007-905320-3**

Printed in Canada, December 2007
REACHING OUR GREATER DESTINY / RANDI DONE

REACHING
OUR GREATER DESTINY

RANDI DONE

PANORAMA PUBLISHING CO.

Dedication

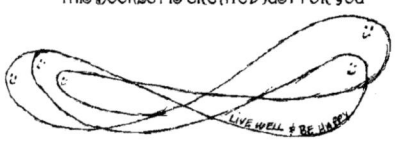

ENJOY THIS LITTLE TREASURE

We share the same heart. We care.

We care about reclaiming the best of ourselves.

We care about peace, harmony and goodwill toward all.

We care about the power required to rise from our own ashes.

We care about life—all life.

Please help me in my caring.

Together we can shift and raise human consciousness.

Together we can heal from our angst, sorrow and suffering.

Together we may unite and harmonize with one good intention,

"Peace on earth and goodwill toward all," and truly begin anew.

From my heart to yours,

Acknowledgments

*

With warmest thanks,
bouquets of gratitude go to
Tommi Hanley, Assistant Editor
Julie Hangasmaa, Graphic Artist, and
Cheryl Forrest, Artist, "Better Than Gold."

Introduction

Mine is a voice calling from the wilderness,
where stillness reigns, long since forgotten.
Is anyone there? Can anyone hear?
Does anyone care?
If you are not there, be present.
If you cannot hear, listen.
If you do not care, care.
Hear this calling.

God is God is God, and by any other name God is still God.

What matters is what something is,
not what it is called.

Some refer to God as Life, Infinite Love, One, Our Creator, Our Father in Heaven, Our Glory Whole, Our Eternal All, Great Spirit, Spirit of the Universe, Sunlight of the Spirit, Absolute Spirit, Divine Creative Intelligence, Universal Mind, Source, The Force, Wise One, Power of Peace, Tao, Parmeshwara, Brahman, Allah and others use God as an acronym to mean Good Orderly Direction. Add to the list...

I use all titles interchangeably as meaning <u>One God</u>, which is of all life centre and from which all life forms a part of our eternal All. When we are centered within ourselves, we become aligned and centered within the mind of God; we not only live with God in our heart, we awaken and begin living within the heart of God.

In writing <u>Reaching Our Greater Destiny</u>, it is my intention to impassion the hearts and minds of everyone to commit to the nobler cause of honouring life, all life, beginning with our own. I hope to inspire individuals everywhere who have lost faith, or who have no faith that works, to commit to a healing journey of spiritual renewal. When we create peace within ourselves, world peace is not only possible it is already on its way.

This book shows through a process of self-examination and maturing thought processes how I suffered and triumphed over my loss of God and returned to a love for all life, including my own. Know thyself. Hopefully this book will be helpful and encourage others to engage in a similar journey of reconnecting with the true self, ultimately with the God self. We may begin this journey by first asking for direction, for help and accepting it when it comes.

The existence of God is a universal idea that has existed cross-culturally and apparently since we drew first breath. We seem to be born with an innate knowingness of God and sense of connection to all. Baby's the world over babble the same at birth. Theirs is a universal language. We only lose this language of origin by adapting to the language of the country where we were born. We are socialized into the customs and traditions of our country and of our generation. We are called to pay close attention to the universal wisdom of what our young children have to teach. We are called to begin loving ourselves with the same protection and care that we would naturally extend to our most vulnerable—to our babies. Their breath and ours depends on this.

When we surrender to love, we begin to create peace within ourselves and, again, world peace becomes not only possible it is already in the making. Yet, for some, engaging in a healing journey of spiritual renewal, and coming to believe in a unifying and loving God of our own understanding is an arduous task. This journey requires each of us to awaken, face and release our greatest fear of all; it is not death, it is our fear of surrendering to love. Because I sense a growing need for individual spiritualism in relationship to the whole of humankind's need for world peace, I encourage everyone to meet and release the fear of love and embrace the courage to live. 13

Paul Henry Thiry D'Holbach wrote in <u>The System of Nature</u>, (1770), "The enlightened man...is capable of pursuing his own happiness...and not to take that for truth upon the authority of others." I am reminded that any healing and spiritual journey is personal, and often requires us to examine ourselves and everything we were hitherto taught. When we seek truth, truth is revealed and as we are able to handle the truth and live truth, more and more truth will be revealed. As we trust in this process, trust in our own truth shivers and trust in our God stuff, we will become more and more responsible and free.

As we remember our best parts, reclaim our lost parts and the gems we threw away, we begin to know, nourish, love and help ourselves grow. As we polish our true self, our God self, we begin to shine and live in partnership with God; we become part of God's glorious journey of creation. As we surrender to love, transformative by its very nature, we satisfy our greatest need of all; it is our need to belong and live useful and purposeful lives knowing we are supporting part of the whole.

As we transform toward inner peace, the whole of humankind will begin to live and make decisions supporting a common vision for world peace, harmony and goodwill toward all, and we will grow in deep human satisfaction. When we contribute to these nobler hopes and dreams, we uplift ourselves and resurrect the whole of humankind; we begin reaching our greater destiny.

We are not so very different, you and I. Indeed, we are similar in key spiritual tenets. United, there is little we cannot accomplish in a host of cooperative ventures; we can live in peace as brothers and sisters world-wide; we can live as a friend among friends.

Since God's work on earth is expressed through our willingness to get involved in the beauty of creation by nurturing and helping to grow our true self, writing Reaching Our Greater Destiny also expresses my willingness to become a co-creator in a host of God's co-operative ventures. And, since a spiritual journey is never ending, I hope you keep what is worth keeping and with the breath of kindness blow the rest away. Enjoy the journey; it's the best ride in life!

P.S.
Today I know nothing! Absolutely nothing! I am a blank page, an empty vessel; transparent, open, restful...it is one of my most contented days.

15

Quotes
The Holy Bible, Jewish Proverbs and The Holy Quaran

*

*"You shall love the Lord your God with all your heart,
and with all your soul, and with all your mind.
The second is like it,
You shall love your neighbour as yourself.
On these two commandments depend all the law and the prophets."*
(Mat 22:37-40)

*"Who is the bravest hero? He who turns his enemy into a friend.
...Judge not thy neighbour until thou art come into his place."*
(Jewish Proverbs)

*Mother Teresa of Calcutta said, "If you judge people,
you have no time to love them."*

*There is no god but God; Muhammad is the messenger of God.
"Even as the fingers of two hands are equal,
so are human beings equal to one another.
No one has any right, nor any preference to claim another.
You are brothers.*
(Final Sermon of Muhammad)

*"...Well, Master, thou hast said the truth:
for there is one God."*
(Mar 12:32)

CONTENTS

Mankinde

No man is an Iland intire of it selfe;
Every man is a peece of the Continent,
A part of the main; if a clod bee washed
Away by the sea,
Europe is the leese, as well as if a
Promontorie were,
As well as if a Mannor of thy friends or of
thine owne were,
Any man's death diminishes me, because I
Am involved in mankinde;
And therefore never send to know for whom
The bell tolls;
It tolls for thee.

—John Donne (1624)

ONE

*God's Barbie Dolls

The longest distance to truth exists between our head and our heart. When we achieve integration, we are enlightened and centered. We become sensitive to the presence of divinity within our own spirit and begin to live in responsive cooperation. Aligned with God, we live in harmony with our soul and are connected to humankind. Making a conscious decision to choose life, by reaching out for help to a life supporting divinity to show us the way, we may listen and be intuitively guided in right action; we begin being part of our eternal All and harmonize with life.

When our head and hearts unite, we will know a great truth. We will begin to live in a spirit of harmony with each other, rather than discord. We will change history and begin reaching toward our greater destiny, one predictable possibility, peace on earth and goodwill toward all. We will stop blaming God and each other, and become responsible and free. Whatever is our differing yet similar beliefs all over the world we can connect with our eternal All, and one by one return to and reclaim the beauty and power that can be found in the truth of our own hearts. We can remember God.

We can awaken to a fierceness of heart made greater in its need to care for and protect life. When we do, the firestorms fast approaching will be expunged and we can loll around on green pastures, eat apples and be grateful that we are alive and breathe today. If war is causally predetermined, so are we, and dolls or not we can change everything when we first change ourselves back to whom we really are; love. Life is freely given to you and me, and we are free to honour life, or not. Before peace comes a call for unity with our Eternal All.

Our Eternal All

Forming part
of our eternal All,
we see...

Forming part
of our eternal All,

we see our part,
and more...

We see clearly,

truth..beauty...love...

We all forming parts
of our eternal All.

Randi Done

As if I see a fire storm fast approaching, I run to you wanting to shake mankind. Daring to disturb the big sleep, I shout, "Wake up! Wake up!" Are we God's Barbie dolls, busily creating atom bombs, robots without moral thinking-checks, and other such genetic Frankenstein mutations? Or, are we fleshy and energetic thinking souls empowered by God's calling for life enhancing free choices? We can stop our impulse to praise God and blame the devil. We can claim personal responsibility over all our individual and collective actions. We can thank God, ourselves and each other because we know we've done our part.

We can make moral decisions by committing to "first do no harm." We must accept that as human beings we can, before making any decision, ask and sense what comes. Just because we can, and are willing…should we? In humility, we must realize that many good intentions have unwanted consequences. We are all responsible for the course humankind charts, and not just a handful of so-called morally enlightened intelligentsia, corporate influences, or the elected. We are called to be conscious and active participants in the creation of our own destiny.

We need not be interminably habituated by a mental inertia that reeks with the swamp-stench of the indolent sins of selfishness, power and control and fearful guilt-ridden cowardice. Our thoughts can stop being intent on war mongering impulses and frog-leaping our future into predictable possibilities, or, worse, into unknown lily galactic pads to pillage and perish. We can open our hearts and listen to the dead, from spaces incomprehensible, voiced in kindness, to our seemingly deaf collective conscience. We can hear their cries to war no more, as they lay in wild fields of daisies, their hearts filled with regret, regret and more regret.

"That mothers shall but smile when they behold
their infants quarter'd with the hands of war," (Caesar III,i, 86)
"And graves have yawned, and yielded up their dead," (Caesar II, I, 69)
wherein they lay in wild fields of daisies their bed,
filled with hearts of regret, regret, and more
REGRET! My blood curdles, "C'est le vie?"

In consideration of the final result, our impartial arbiter calls us to choose which side of the fence we are willing to exit or grow toward, "Are we energy haters and energy lovers, thereby destined toward reciprocal annihilation? Or, will our god-given instinct to survive and cherish life, all life, quantum leap in triumph? As two opposing Masters, we cannot both serve and survive. "To be, or not to be: that is the [only] question" (Shakespeare, Hamlet III, i). This is our one free choice, and this choice presents itself to us in everyway, everyday.

Perhaps my thoughts were so preoccupied with war that I had become diseased. Looking back, festering away were decades of memories fraught with violence, personal and global. Suffering and squirming in a false sense of powerlessness, I sank deeper and deeper into the dark abyss. On the brink of my own demise, it took years of honest introspection to release what I've come to refer to as the inner-terrorist.

I needed to detach from all my suffering (mostly self-imposed). I needed to become willing to shift away from all preconceived notions, beliefs and perceptions that I might adopt a positive attitude toward everything and everyone, including myself. Whether from a personal or a global perspective, we must all answer the question, "Which Master am I willing to serve—life or death?"

The consequences are nasty when we continue to think and act as our forefathers. We must answer the question, "Is war causally pre-determined by an unbroken

29

chain of prior occurrences, or can we change the course of history, end all killing and start living in unity?" We are not God's Barbie dolls bending to his almighty will. We are thinking and feeling human beings, capable of caring and rising from all that is exterior to our moral law within.

We are called to rise from our ashes and angst and choose anew. As it stands, not unlike the evil atrocities committed under the leadership of Hitler, individual justification for war crimes appears to be, "I was just following orders!" When we deny our own sense of what is right, true, virtuous and good, we disconnect from self honesty and personal loathing settles within.

Before acquiescing to the will of a political leader (who may have won a democratic election only marginally), we can be true to our conscience and ask ourselves, "Can I kill someone today?" The answer may be, "Yes, I can!" Then we may ask, "Am I willing to kill someone today?" Again, we can answer any moral question with, "Can I" and "Am I willing?" Check within and sense what comes. This is the beginning of individual integrity, personal responsibility and self respect.

We deserve the possibility of knowing planetary peace, joy and goodwill amongst all human life.

The hard life of misery and martyrdom can end. We can clearly state, "I just don't feel like killing anyone today. I don't need to explain, rationalize or justify that decision. I just don't feel like it today and you can't make me. Tomorrow, who knows, but not today." We deserve personal peace of mind. In unison we can call out to each other, "Let us run from war and walk together in peace."

We can remember the courage of the Vietnam War draft dodgers. True to themselves, they were willing to risk everything, even being disowned by their families. They followed the dictates of their own conscience and can never be accused of gross disrespect toward human life because they were, "just following orders." Despite being called anarchists, traitors, betrayers and worse, could the solution, "I just don't feel like killing anyone today, and you can't make me" be just that simple for everyone, everywhere? We can remember our brave, salute their courage to care for and protect life, and again we can march for peace.

The unwillingness to war is the sane thought that can save and prevent us all from going under, horribly, suffocating in the foul earthy trenches, and all the long while internally revolting from it. No doubt, politicians everywhere might consider me mad and radical for even suggesting such a simplistic solution to voters everywhere. Scandalous anarchy could reign, resulting in rebellious non-compliance everywhere. Good grief and Heavens-to-Betsy, "Whatever may become of us? Peace at last?" Shall we continue to lace up and march off to war? Or, just fly around in the dark and drop bombs upon the innocent? Ask, and sense what comes, "Has our own watch stopped, or are we just running out of time?"

As for one of the Ten Commandments, "Thou shalt not kill," one must wonder how just wars are, and how just are the men who are wearing the pants in the family who fight in war? Does the bible say, "Thou shalt not kill unless provoked or feeling threatened? Or, thou shalt not kill unless I'm scared of losing something I have, or of not getting something I want? Or, thou shalt not kill unless it's a pre-emptive strike?" The commandment simply and clearly states, "Thou shalt not kill."

After all, the big 'they' might be thinking of attacking us...so, let's attack first to show them who is boss. And, while we're at it, let's get England and Europe involved too. One must wonder, "Where is the connection between national self interests, world-wide religions and global political will?" Regardless of nation or religious preference, the time is now for women to lead the world toward peace, wearing pants or not; we can introduce spiritual solutions to political problems and ask our men to lace up their marching boots and walk in peace. We win when we unite.

Whatever are our differing religious or political beliefs, the time is ripe that we unite in the worthy goal of choosing love over hate, and life over death. Otherwise, the predictable outcome of continually succumbing to anything other than peaceful impulses will be that none of our best interests will be met or protected. Witnessing this ongoing plunge into deep moral kah-kah, some of us may continue lamenting, "Father, forgive them; for they know not what they do" (Luk 23:34).

As passionate about world peace as Pope John Paul II, I also call out to people everywhere, "No more war...No more war...Repent!" Since we are all in the same sandbox called Earth, we must 'play nice.' But since Joey stuck a stick in Sally's eye, Sally got Billy to stick a stick in Joey's eye. Then Joey knocked out Billy's front teeth, and Sally felt compelled to knock out Joey's teeth. A huge fracas erupts and Joey's brother knocks down Billy and Sally's sand castles, the 'twin towers.' Next thing you know everyone is 'pissed' and there's blood everywhere. Nobody is having fun and there's no other sandbox to go play in; so now what do we do? Pope John Paul II, also cried out to the world, "You are my hope. You give me hope!"

> *When we listen to the cries from those who love humanity, we remember, "Any man's death diminishes me, because I am involved in mankinde" (John Donne).*
>
> *We know that when we strike out against another, we are energetically striking out against ourselves and harming our collective unit. We strike God!*

Does behavior supporting resolving conflicts such as is found in <u>The Holy Bible</u>, "Ye heard that it has been said, An eye for an eye, and a tooth for a tooth:" (Mat 5:38) continue to justify our actions? If insanity can be defined as doing the same thing over and over again and expecting a different result is true, when will the insanity of war end? Clearly, to continue as we have, historical results will remain the same. To war is to die. To support life, is to live a life of peace; revenge is a solution that promises unhappy consequences.

Yet we continue to seek human morality and kinship with God in text, biblical and otherwise. Instead, we may surrender to love and experience a personal relationship with our true self in connection with our eternal All.   34

Interestingly, when we find God we also find supporting evidence of God everywhere, including in text, biblical and otherwise.

The answers will come when we ask the right questions, ask for help and ask for direction. We will ask the right question when we connect with how we are feeling and what it is that we need and how it is that we can be most helpful. We do not need to think our way to a solution; we need only to pose the question. It is when we acknowledge that we feel scared-to-death by the possibility of global extinction that we will want to know how to satisfy our need to feel safe and cared for in a world that appears to be anything but, and to begin to create atmospheres of global harmony motivated by love for self, our children and future generations. We will understand that in the final analysis, love, also eternal and freely given without expectation, for love is its own reward, is all that matters and makes our lives worthy of remembering.

> *We may remember that our every action is an expression of love, or a call for unity. By committing ourselves to one noble cause, in unity we can accomplish great things; Peace on earth and goodwill toward all.*

It Matters

It matters
  not the most
    the amount of time
      we have on earth.

It matters most
  the love we share
    that marks its lasting worth.
      ~Randi Done

When I connected with my own fears and insecurities, I realized the only way I would ever feel safe in the world is if I began to feel safe within myself. To do that, I needed to go back in time and review my personal history to understand where, when and how I became disconnected, defensive and self destructive in life. The goal was to return to my original state of being at birth, one of complete connection between self, God and humankind.

How the process of integration would happen was beyond my rational scope. Nonetheless, I trusted and placed complete reliance on its possibility. Far too much to handle on my own, this Barbie doll asked for guidance and it came, in spades, but not until I asked for help. "And all things, whatsoever ye shall ask in prayer, believing, ye shall receive" (Mat 21:22).

Therefore, we must be very careful what we pray for, what is our intention and our motivation, what visions of desire we send out into the atmospheric plane, because that is what shall become manifest in our lives. Life is manifest as belief personified. If our external reality is a reflection of our inner reality, and we don't like what we see exterior to us we must change within.

> *We can dare to dream the big dream, our best dream—peace at last! We can imagine it. See it. Hear it. Feel and experience it. We can know peace, be peace and be guided by peace. We can believe in the dream promising the happiest, most joyful and harmonious outcome for all. This inner reality will manifest a new world peace.*

When we believe and are committed to creating a safe haven on Earth as in Heaven, peace becomes more than possible. It is already in the making. All that is required is that we show up for the day and simply do the best we can by consciously committing to and being willing to do whatever it takes to first create peace within ourselves.

It appears that only humankind has the ability to willfully resist the impulse to glorify ourselves, and to be bent on self-destructing by succumbing to the urgings of our inner-terrorist. It is that critical and negating voice within that seeks to take us down, keep us down and take the individual and humankind out, permanently. Having been somewhat tarnished by the darker sides of life, many years of battling with my own inner-terrorist, it was a long loop-de-loop before I attempted to resurrect myself. Suffering is the great teacher and motivator. We may all begin reaching toward all that is our human potential—inner peace. I ask, "Why build these cities glorious, if man unbuilded goes" (Edwin Markham: Man Making)?

Born to emigrant parents from Norway, I grew up on a cattle ranch near a remote logging community in north-central British Columbia. It was from the native population, soft spoken and gentle people, whose heightened sensitivity and reverence toward life seemed to lift me to the place where stillness reigns. Silence. Listening. Being. The natives seem to have a sense of peace borne of acceptance, gratitude and trust in the Great Spirit. Since I consider my home town a microcosm of the world, I am encouraged by everyone's healing journey of spiritual renewal; Anglo-Saxon Christian's and Natives alike, we remember and reclaim our true spiritual identity.

This sense of spirituality I also find in the cyclical solstices of nature, wherein exists a balanced and symbiotic system of relationship between all living things; and all seemingly for the sole purpose of each part supporting the whole, and each living thing growing toward its full genetic potential prior to death. Somehow even the dying of things is as poignantly beautiful as the first shoots of spring. There exists the beauty of necessity even in death, even for a single blade of grass.

However, peace was not always present; it was often absent and resulted in unnecessary death. Mixing booze with feelings of anger, jealousy and all sorts of slights, can soon ignite and unleash within a contemptible vile that manifests in amoral action, violence and tragic death. Stabbed, shot to death at point-blank range, drowning and all sorts of horrendous beatings became blended in with nature's calm. Such as war, what was going on in our own backyard was often ignored. Yet, our sun, a life giver itself, continued to shine as brightly on death as it does on life — waiting, waiting, waiting for us to 'get it.'

Without discrimination to race, colour or the amount of dollars in the bank, feelings of remorse, sorrow, shame and regret follow in the aftermath of our wrongs against self and others, and for some this downward spiral toward the hell of our own making is often choked back by more booze.

To foster empathy, I grew up with the expression, "Before you judge, walk a mile in my moccasins." We are reminded of the importance that it is our lost and suffering souls who offer us the 'opportunity' to provide understanding, encouragement and support. Still, it was the familiar face of trauma that scarred the hearts in our otherwise idyllic community; it became the unspoken expression of our everyday reality.

Yet, in nature we may find a place for healing, and we may always return to the place where stillness reigns and say to ourselves, "Be still, and know that I am God" (Psalm 46:10). The source of our unhappiness rests in our ignorance of nature. We humans must choose to create symbiotic systems of relationship between all living things; we humans have free will. We can focus only on the positive and help it to grow, or we can focus on what's lacking and wither. We can create our happiest outcomes by committing to the idea that united there is little we cannot do for the benefit of all. We can begin by asking, not what the world can do for us but what we can do for the freedom of man. We can commit to doing our part in supporting the whole; we will be set free; we will know harmony and peace.

Bringing the individual down to our right size, we are all an extraordinary blade of grass capable of flourishing in the greenest of green fields that is humankind. One blade of grass is of no greater or lesser importance than the blade we grow beside, within the field from which we all form a part.

It only seems to be humankind that is out of balance with nature and out of step, or alignment, with a presumably god-given instinct to be all that we were intended. "Why is that?" I pondered. We humans wither in negativity and flourish in atmospheres of love.   43

> *By surrendering to love, we satisfy our need to feel safe and part of the whole. We begin creating atmospheres of global harmony between self, nature and nations.*

Socrates declared, "The unexamined life is not worth living," and so I examine my life and begin to remember and know my true self.

Prior to and at birth, still in moments of divine connection to all, I also knew that everything that had existed, would exist, did exist in a split second of totality and that this totality could alter with one voice, with one massive global shift in perception. At birth, as in death, I also traveled through a tunnel of light and became one with super-gravity. Traveling the distance between here and there is so fast that time and space seems to stand still, which is no distance at all. I remember.

I distinctly recall the feelings and thoughts I had the day I discovered my body, and that I was in it. At 11 months, laying on my back, just waking up, it was as if I saw my leg for the first time. So, I twisted my ankle, played with my fingers and hands, and simply marveled at the connection between mind and body. That was power! This entire awareness was wonderful and I knew that from that moment on, I had not only arrived, I was the boss of my body and its movements.

I also remember closing my eyes and seeing everything that I was destined to experience while living on Earth. "Here we go," I groaned with some resignation, knowing that much of it would be painful and very challenging, and that it would be nip'n tuck if I'd 'get it' while alive. I had not chosen the easy road, but knew that the resulting growth would be for my benefit and for the benefit of others. I also knew that when I opened my eyes, that I would forget everything. I would forget my map. It was with some comfort though, that I knew one day I would return to the place from where I had come — my true home of origin.

The next major memory was when I was told I was the boss of my mind. Therein began my difficulty in reconciling the freedom to choose with the knowledge that I had a destiny. It was late spring and I was 23 months old. Sitting on the front porch by my dad, with a dolly in my arms, we posed while waiting for mom to figure out how to use the camera. I remember thinking, "You'd have to be God to get the big picture. God is kind 'a like that camera. It can see everything, everywhere, all the time. Unlike the camera, God is also in everything, everywhere, all the time, at once." This thought blew me away. I peed my pants.

Feeling a bit frightened and small in this suddenly great big world, holding onto my small dolly, I asked, "Daddy? Am I God's dolly?" My Dad caught his breath and said something along the lines, "That's a big question for such a little girl. I'll have to think about that one." After a brief pause he continued, "Have you ever noticed spiders? See that one over there? See the spider web? It's stronger than steal. The mommy spider can create a thousand tiny baby spiders. I think if you want to know about God, you have to pay close attention to the miracles that are happening all around you, everyday." I pressed on, "Daddy am I your dolly?"

My dad, always a strong believer in the power of his mind, said something to the effect, "The mind is an amazing thing. You have to discipline it. You'd better change the way you're thinking or you'll get yourself into trouble. It's your conscience you come face-to-face with, so you'd better like what you see in the mirror. What I do know is that you're my princess. You'll always be my princess." Of course, I didn't have a clue what he was talking about.   46

Me and Dad
Eugen Georg, Christmas, 2006

My mom never liked it when dad was so serious with me. When she asked what we were talking about, we both just shrugged and dad fibbed, saying, "Oh, nothing much," and then we smiled and said, "Cheese" for the camera. Reconciling the fact that we have a destiny and that we also have freedom of choice, both concepts have been wrestling for dominance in my mind from age 23 months until almost age 50. In any event, I wisely stopped talking and asking questions for at least one year.

At 33 months, I started to lose connection with my own light. Some of the more unsavoury aspects of life began to occur, and my life became forever altered. At birth we have knowingness that we are all the sons and daughters of one God. But this sense of oneness is often kyboshed due to our inability to reconcile the bad things that happen in our life with belief systems that preach about a loving and merciful God. It is then that we shift from a state of connection to disconnection from self, people and from God. We may become lost in chaos and fear, which is non-conducive to creating peace on Earth as in Heaven...

We all experience the impact of trauma; the world is full of it. For some, watching the news causes nightmares. Not only in war torn countries, there are all sorts of moral boundary-breaking and human rights violations that happen everywhere. The good news is that we can recover from trauma and flourish when we commit to a healing journey of spiritual renewal.

For many, healing begins when enough suffering brings us to our knees and in humility we cry out for help. We may listen to an inner pulse for life made greater in its need for life itself, and hear our wise one plea, "Physician, heal thyself." Believing we can be made whole, we will heal.

When we become ready to listen and receive divine help, we will help ourselves and be intuitively directed to people and circumstances that will help. We will shift beyond the realm of self and into a sphere of wholeness. We will lift from Hell and return to love for life.   48

Always the solution to any difficulty we can surrender to love, ask for help and heal. When we become willing to receive love, we open a gateway for miracle-making. We become miraculous examples of love's transformative nature, with a growing capacity for compassion, acceptance and loving-kindness.

When we begin to remember former moments of genuine joy, we realize that God never abandoned us; rather, we abandoned God. We can renew our personal relationship with God, just as we do in any meaningful relationship—with an open heart and honest dialogue.

When we have conversations with God, to listen is our highest expression of respect. When we do, we can start co-participating in our own transformation. We are blessed, because we have entered a journey of loving guidance, understanding and forgiveness, and we are set free.

We will begin to notice that the right people show up at exactly the right time; we notice we are on a path of healing and synchronicity. We begin to hear what we need to hear, and we feel heard. We start to feel what we need to feel. We start to let go, and we heal. As our perceptions, emotions and thoughts shift, we begin to feel safe and loved by a universe supporting of our commitment to heal. We start to realize that God works through people who are willing to help and to be helped. We begin to trust in life.

Dad was right. The mind is amazing. We not only need to discipline it, but our minds will protect us. We will not remember until we are willing to heal and become strong enough to handle the truth. Illusions vanish when we became strong enough to ask to be helped to see the truth. Painlessly and effortlessly, we are divinely helped. God will do for us what we cannot do for ourselves—reveal truth. We will remember everything, glazed with calming balm and we are set free. Traumas are part of our map; the map we forgot. Our map is our destiny and traumas are part of it. With a positive spin, one might consider traumas as being intended for our spiritual evolution.

We can adopt an attitude that helps us accept everyone's humanness and necessity to err that we can advance in our abilities to forgive.

We can accept our map, our destiny and trust that good can come from what is life destroying. This is no easy task, it is for the courageous. For example, at age nine, in a dusty attic of an abandoned building, I accepted the spiritual teachings of Jesus Christ into my heart; when I adopt the principles of love, compassion and forgiveness into application of every possible set of circumstances, they are my saving grace. Two weeks later I was raped by a sixteen-year-old boy in a foreign country, who also threatened to harm my three-year-old sister if I told. I didn't. Curious timing…

Having no forgiveness in my heart, I entered a field of hateful fantasy, with him tarred, feathered and strung up for public display and vicious judgmental condemnation. I had murder in my heart until I forgot that too. Much later, I heard this young man had a very unhappy life. At first I felt smug and thought, "Justice has been served." Within seconds, I felt sad for him and thought, "What a wasted life—his and mine." I entered a field of compassion and wished only good things for him. From a distance, I brought his spirit energy to my minds eye and flooded him with light and love. I was freed.

I started to remember everything. Searching for truth, including knowledge of what my part was, I recalled a specific moment. As I ran up the rickety stairs of an old barn (we were playing hide and seek), I clearly heard, "Go back." I paused and looking backward, I thought "What was that? How odd." I continued racing up the stairs, ignored my intuitive voice and all hell broke loose. Someone said to me once, "If it's odd, it's God!"

Reflecting deeper on the subject of destiny, divinity and intuitive guidance, I recall Jesus had priori knowingness that Judas would betray him. Jesus also ignored his intuitive forewarning. Many of us participate in our own undoing. Goes does not forsake us; yet, despite the life-saving value of intuition, it seems some of us are called to suffer and sacrifice that others might later be helped and saved.

Often it is our walking wounded who later become healers, a source of inspiration, hope and helpfulness to others. A healing journey of spiritual renewal blossoms when we connect with a loving Creator, and begin to remember and reclaim our true self, our innocence and love for life — all life. Knowing that everywhere there are stories of triumph over trauma and that victory is possible for casualties of war and all manner of human aggression, we have cause for hope. We may begin to remember love. Mine is such a journey, and so I continue to remember the good and grow the good.

At age four, in celebration of May Day, I was one of a handful of little fairies happily dancing around our Queen. I was wearing the prettiest blue silk dress. With a woven basket full of rose petals, intended for tossing at the feet of our May Day Queen, it was our community's annual expression of joy for life and hope for renewal.

But, I ran out of petals. Seeing so many laying on the floor, I dove to the floor and with an all encompassing scoop gathered up as many petals as I could and began tossing them all over us little fairies. I somehow knew that not only should the May Day Queen be showered in petals, but that we are all cause for celebration and form part of God's infinite expressions of beauty and joy. With that realization I scooped up an even bigger pile of petals, tossing them into the audience and all over myself too.

The following summer, my dad took me to a spot that he later referred to as The Glory Hole. It is an old mining site near Pinchi Lake. He left me in the car as he walked off to prospect for gems, possibly jade. On this scorching day, inquisitive and fearless as usual, I did a little exploration of my own. I discovered this huge hole in the ground. It was scary because I could have fallen through. I wisely lay flat on my stomach and sidled as near to the hole as possible.

Peering into the darkness, I began dropping pebbles into the hole. Listening intently for sounds of my little rocks hitting a bottom, I heard none. "Wow!" I thought, "What if this pebble travels all the way through to the other side of the earth? What if someone in China sees it popping out at the other end and catches it? We could play catch. Wouldn't it be something if we could all connect? That's magic!"

Peering deeper into black holes and baby universes, as a child I could easily speculate on possibilities and points of creation. I speculated that people were like particles of light, perhaps stardust, popping out the other side transformed as human. Conversely, fascinated by stars, I could similarly imagine being human and then popping out the other side transformed as a star. As a child, I was a skinny kid with a big imagination. I still believe that if we can imagine a thing, believing it makes it so; we gravitate to evidence that supports Truth. Life is a wonder, a magical and mysterious phenomenon; a beauty to behold and I am in the eye of the beholder. I remember.

Not much later, I was so excited when I discovered infinity. I ran into the house wanting to tell my mom that I could not only count to one hundred, but that I had discovered this incredible secret. Not unlike The Glory Hole, it occurred to me that zero was a very interesting curiosity, and not really a number at all. Yet, somehow that zero was the critical and necessary connection for all numbers to connect with all numbers, backward and forward numbers, and maybe even looping numbers.

Again, I speculate on possibilities that God is centre for infinite points of creation and from which all transformations of energy, of life itself flows to and from Our Glory Whole; together we form parts of this glorious whole and timeless flow of life. Constantly redefining who I am and my place in the universe, I remember infinity.

My imagination just took off...flying into the universe. I became so caught up in the mystery of numbers. They became like the dancing of the seven veils, like silk easily catching the air, its fabric flowing softly with ease and grace throughout time, all connected and integrated as one. They became like silvery strands ever so gently interweaving within its full spectrum of light — shimmering with all colours of the rainbow. But the pot of gold is not out there, somewhere, at the end of the rainbow. Such as a kaleidoscope racing...it all came back to me. I knew the pot of gold is found within. Life is a grand prism of light and we are its golden spark of life divine.

But, my mom and dad had company, so I never did get around to sharing this magic—this really big secret. Anyway, sometimes big people are guilty of not believing that young children or little babies have big people thoughts. Or maybe big people just forget their best thoughts. I did. The good news is we can end our search for God and remember Truth within.

As a kid, sometimes I'd play cards and loved it when I got the deuce; the wild card—the good luck card giving me an edge to a winning hand. I remember thinking, I wonder if God is like the wild card...yet the only difference is that we can say, "Hey, I need a wild card...and just get it." Perhaps this good luck card is determinism's missing link that links us all, and appears as wholly random accidentals that synchronizes within the willing a healing journey of spiritual renewal. With this ever present gift that waits for us to call, perhaps when we do we can co-create our own luck, and all of us enjoy a winning hand in humankind's course in miracle making.

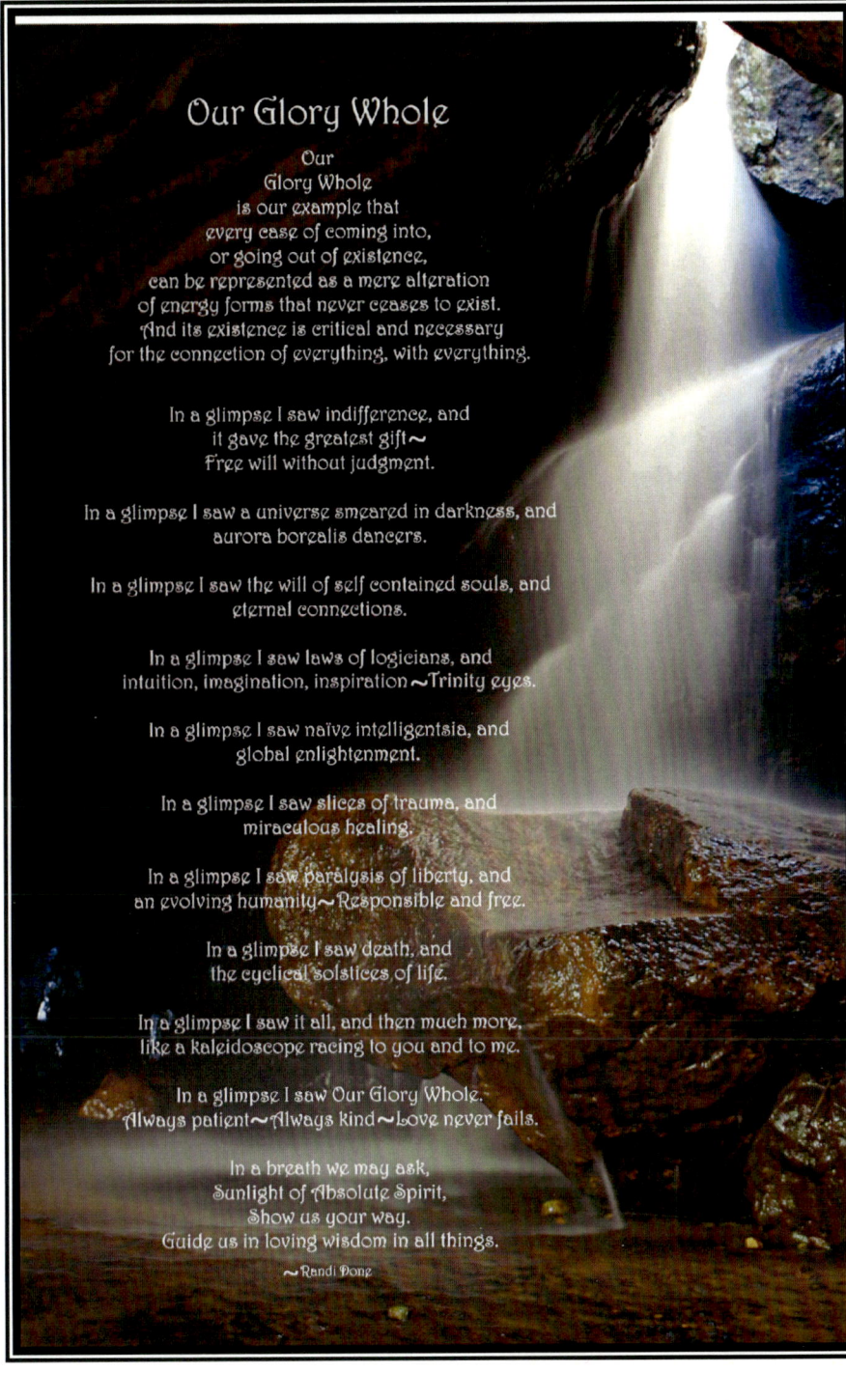

Our Glory Whole

Our
Glory Whole
is our example that
every case of coming into,
or going out of existence,
can be represented as a mere alteration
of energy forms that never ceases to exist.
And its existence is critical and necessary
for the connection of everything, with everything.

In a glimpse I saw indifference, and
it gave the greatest gift~
Free will without judgment.

In a glimpse I saw a universe smeared in darkness, and
aurora borealis dancers.

In a glimpse I saw the will of self contained souls, and
eternal connections.

In a glimpse I saw laws of logicians, and
intuition, imagination, inspiration ~Trinity eyes.

In a glimpse I saw naïve intelligentsia, and
global enlightenment.

In a glimpse I saw slices of trauma, and
miraculous healing.

In a glimpse I saw paralysis of liberty, and
an evolving humanity~Responsible and free.

In a glimpse I saw death, and
the cyclical solstices of life.

In a glimpse I saw it all, and then much more,
like a kaleidoscope racing to you and to me.

In a glimpse I saw Our Glory Whole.
Always patient~Always kind~Love never fails.

In a breath we may ask,
Sunlight of Absolute Spirit,
Show us your way.
Guide us in loving wisdom in all things.
~Randi Done

Better Than Gold

Like the mystery of angels

and colours sublime,

we are dancing silk

in mystical time.

§

Like golden beams

in magical rhyme,

we are rays of light

sparkling in kind.

§

Better than gold,

intended to shine,

We are bits of a rainbow's

exquisite design.

§

Transforming within,

our radiance divine,

we are love for each other,

for all humankind.

~ Randi Done

Once, while sitting under the kitchen table, thumb-sucking for comfort from fear of a most powerful and torrential rainstorm, I spontaneously jumped out from under, peeled off my clothes, raced outside and in the darkness did multitudes of cartwheels in the rain. Illuminated only by streaking bolts of lightening, it is with great joy that I recollect the feeling of being inextricably part of it all. I feel most glorified when I surrender to being part of One who has all power.

Perhaps when I entertain the simplicity of such ideas as the necessity to surrender to win, it is a bit wild and unconventional. Not surprising to know, therefore, that I used to love running around naked whenever I could get away with it. My favourite place in the wilderness was on old game trails found at the top of Dickinson's Hill. From these peaks I could scan the village below and far beyond. I could speculate on possibilities of peace without dividing lines in the sand. I could imagine unity of thought and purpose that stems from evolved individual spiritualism; One God. One People. One life; we are an integral part of life and are of intrinsic value to each other. We can surrender and unite.

When it was windy, there was a poplar tree in our front yard that I liked to climb. It was just the perfect size to bend with my weight. I would happily sway back and forth with ease and grace. When I played my favourite game on rainy days, which was to spin the globe with my eyes closed and see where I'd land. I'd wonder about the people who lived there, what they ate and did for fun. I just wanted to know and become friends with everybody, and wondered if they played 'spin the globe,' too, or if they even had a globe to spin. When I wasn't climbing mountains and trees, or swimming and splashing with great gusto and glee, I loved lolling around and watch cloud formations change by the hour, and day dream about the big picture. And, I need to go back further...

Sometimes mom would ask, "When are you going to grow up?" I'd think, "What does that mean? Mmm...could that mean accepting personal responsibility for the consequences of all our choices, and being sensitive to and mindful of how our choices might impact the lives of others?" Or, does the epitome of personal responsibility rest in a resolve to be true to our own source of intuitive guidance...our highest form of intelligence?

However, when God answered me through my own intuition, if it didn't make sense, I hung up the phone. So, I not only need to stop finger pointing and let everyone off the hook, I need to make restitution and change my ways. I need to listen, trust and act on the wisdom of a guidance that sees and knows far more than I. I need to surrender my ego and open to universal mind.

With zero connection to my sense of inner knowingness, or God presence, it was always difficult for me to make decisions. I lived within the constraints of a conflicted and uncertain soul as to what was the right choice. My mom used to say, "Randi, listen to your heart. Follow your heart." And, my dad used to say, "God gave you a brain. Use it." Whenever I needed to make a decision, often my heart and mind were in conflict. How I felt and what I thought about a situation did not often jive, and both felt wrong, or half right.

Mom also used to say, "Randi, work with what you have and help it grow," and "Just be you and everything will work out." What she didn't realize, nor I, was that I didn't know who I was. Painfully and often with disappointing results, I attempted to live life by being someone I thought others wanted or needed me to be. Without self knowledge, I wore many masks and the concept "To thine own self be true" seemed a selfish ideal. I was wrong.

Prior to reaching a place where I have a genuine desire to surrender every morning, open to knowing how I can be helpful, I was fraught with self-doubt and relied heavily on external validation. When my mother failed me, I turned to the church for guidance to help me make an important life decision. The minister leaned back in his chair, and smiled one of those "I know something you don't, you poor sweet suffering soul," and then he said, "Not your will, Randi, but God's be done," and "You've got to row your own boat!" I crudely thought, "Well, what the hell does that mean?"

Baffled and angered, I left the office fuming, "If only I did have power! I'd toss steeples across nations, like dice bouncing across a crap table!" Confused, I behaved like a victim in life and the world owed me a favour. I sought guidance, but left my true self out of the equation.

Besides needing to lighten-up, forgive myself for vacillated years of a life half-lived, I also need to let God, the church and my mother off the hook. I took their patient, kind, nourishing source of support and neutral attitude as being indifferent. When I would ask, "What do you think I should do...advise me...?" Mom, God and church seemed to have the same attitude, "Randi, I cannot live your life for you. You have to live your own life." Today, I am thankful. I am my own best parent, and try to treat myself tenderly as if I were a delicate spring from life.

It was a long journey to become centered, to trust and rely on my own source of inner knowingness. So fearful was I of making mistakes. But, there are no mistakes, only growing pains. It seems to me that whether we realize it or not, we are all engaged in a spiritual process and are exactly where we are supposed to be at any given moment.

I resolve internal conflicts when I remember that decisions based on feelings alone will often betray us, and decisions based on our mind and thinking powers alone will often deceive us; But, decisions based on intuition will never fail us, and upon that I have come to trust and place complete reliance; it is that excited 'yes' feeling within. When I fail to act on intuition my life goes to Hell in-a-hand-basket, fast! When I listen, there exists harmony with my destiny — perfect timing. Thank God, love is long-suffering and waits for us to 'get it' without judgment.

It is suffering that is instigator to change. At this time in history, we are at a precipice of massive global change. If fear must be our motivator, it seems we are at a moment when we are as afraid of change as we are afraid of staying the same. It is a good time to become centered with self, and trust in one God who loves this planet and all people; it's up to us to ask, "What can I do for humankind?" We can ask, sense what comes, trust in guidance and suffer no more. We can unite and win.

When we surrender to love, we step toward the hitherto unknown regions of spiritual bliss.

We feel understood and not judged. We feel kindness when we suffer from our own errors in judgment.

We feel compassion and an unfaltering hope that we will find our way out of the darkness and step into the truth of our own light.

When we surrender to love, we awaken and willingly participate in cooperation and harmony with all. We become life's offering—our best selves.

Knowledge of God's will is another kettle of fish. For example, when I was nine, I wanted proof of God's existence—a loving God. I started talking to this God I didn't particularly believe in and bargained, "If you help me find a four leaf clover, I'll believe you exist." Since I'd already spent hours sprawling around on the green grass, I thought it would be a safe bet there'd be no response. Surprisingly, within seconds, there it was—a perfect four leaf clover. "Mmmm," I mused, "Isn't that interesting?" We can talk to a God we don't know, or believe in, and watch what happens; soon we come to believe that we are cared for and heard.

Considering I had recently been violated, I wondered about God, the big map and God's will for my life. Although I had a brief glimpse of a future promising happy moments of triumph, there was no real clarity or forthcoming answer, so I dawdled off to join the others for dinner.

I don't have a clue about 'God's will.' It is a guessing game at best. I try to accept life as it is and do my best with what's in front of me. I only know that I feel most grateful when I'm able to live in a spirit of helpfulness, sharing and caring with others...when I'm in the 'love flow.' Therefore, my personal relationship with God/life/self begins each morning with a ritual of writing a letter to God, prayer, meditation and a spiritual reading. I surrender, connect, open and relax into the present—which is our gift. 66

Sadly, for many the world over it's difficult to relax into a full and thankful heart when we are warring, sick and poor, hungry and fighting for our very survival. It is difficult to trust the map. Yet, we can trust that God is the spirit of goodwill calling within us all. We also seem to be called to 'float on faith' until we witness and experience the presence of love and its grace in action through us humans.

I'm grateful for peace of mind. When I end the battle within, inner peace grows and I begin to flourish. Leaving my way, the hard way, I now know the importance of trusting intuition. It is the path of ease and grace. At first by a whisper we are guided. With practice this inner knowingness becomes loud and clear, and we fill with wonder and gratitude. Fully committed to a healing journey of spiritual renewal, I work hard for peace.

We will know and accept the path of our destiny, at every moment, by trusting in our intuition. This happens when we are willing to connect with the direct link that exists between our eternal and divine spark of life within, our individual spirit, with the living light and presence of all that is life enhancing—Absolute Spirit. With a genuine desire to be free from all that is blocking us from the sunlight of Absolute Spirit, our souls will propel us to solicit forgiveness for ourselves and others—that we may be free.

Intuition is the reward of connection between the heart and mind...breath...life...spirit.

Intuition is grace in action, and upon this guide we can place complete reliance. Its application is for purposes promising the highest good.

Intuition is our divine link with an all seeing, all knowing, and all protecting infinite source of life enhancing energy. It is our direct link between God and self; the chain may lengthen but it never breaks.

When we consciously choose to receive from an infinite source of love, we have no choice but to become expressers of love. Our great reward will be nothing less than a return to innocence, bliss— elixirs of joy.

Our source of infinite love, light and positive energy resides in the centre of us all. This infinite source of all that is nourishing, we are connected to and we are part of.

When we listen to the holy spirit of intuition, we are guided by infinite wisdom and its perfect care.

We need only listen. We need only say, "Hello. Welcome." We can sing to our centre, "You can relax now. C'mon and open your heart. I'm with you now and I love you." We can listen as our centre sings to us, "This little light of mine, I'm going to let it shine," and the two are united.

Thus began my journey in trying to know, see, go backwards in time to heal, release and understand where, when and how I became disconnected from God, people and more...from myself. It was then that I began the often painful process of re-integration between my head and my heart. I started to thaw. I started to feel. I started to heal.

> *When we surrender to love, we grow closer to our former knowingness of oneness with an all encompassing, all pervasive truth—God is love. We not only begin living with God in our hearts, we begin living within the heart of God.*

In any event, I never did like playing with Barbie dolls. Other girls did. Perhaps being more of a free spirit and non-conformist, I liked to play outside, get dirty and have fun. I especially liked to go fishing with my best friend, Teresa. Sitting beside her on a log that straddled the creek, as we dangled our legs and skimmed our toes across the cool ripples below, we felt at peace and happy To Be. 69

Trying to fit tight clothes onto unwilling and ridged dolls seemed like a complete waste of time. Unlike people filled with vibrancy, breath and the ability to choose to be guided by intuition, Barbie dolls have no free will. We must bend them to our will. They are incapable of changing their mould by consciously choosing to participate in their own transformation. We can. We can choose love, and cheerfully capitalize on our ability to consciously detach from all that exists in opposition to life's eternal values. We can connect, in spiritual cooperation, and become willing to listen to our ever present moral law within—intuitive guidance.

Awestruck by an incredible sense of perfect timing in all things, together with our willingness to connect with God's desire to help, we will be helped. We will conquer our demons and battle within; we can end our habituation to war and return to peace. We can change how we perceive ourselves and our place in the universe. We can know that written on the hearts of stars and ours that we are being guided toward peace on earth as in heaven; we are reaching our greater destiny.

It is not our fear of war and its nasty consequences that has been directing our actions and fates. Nor is it our fear of death, because our action to war negates that premise. It is our fear of love that is our greatest fear in need of overcoming. Surrendering to love, to an absolute unknown on faith alone, is to leave ourselves naked, vulnerable and as powerless as a newborn child is our greatest fear. However, when we surrender to love, open our hearts to love and trust love, we begin to embrace love as the solution to every possible set of circumstances. We redirect our actions and create fates resplendent in satisfying our greater need; it is our need to feel part of and to belong. Trust in the process and evolution of love, and in our longing for God and life itself; it breathes us.

If you are suffering, I can assure you there is cause for hope. There is light at the end of the tunnel and this light exists in the centre of us all. This light is love; it is life itself.

We shorten the distance to truth when our heart and mind unite in remembrance of spirit. Reclaiming the presence of spirit within, we begin to know self—our true self. Our search for truth is rewarded when we remember with admiring awe what always was, what is and what will always be; we remember truth, our eternal self and our perfect placement in the wondrous unfolding of the universe. As creations of life we remember spirit, connect with our Creator within, and we unite in an intention to create world peace and harmony with life—all life.

> *When we surrender to love, we experience fruit borne of faith; "The fruit of the spirit is love, joy, peace, long suffering, gentleness, goodness, faith," (Gal 5:22).*
>
> *Living these truths, we experience the kingdom of heaven within. Enlightened by our maturing love for humanity we begin living as a friend among friends, knowing we all form part of our eternal All.*

P.S.

Just a guess, but, as for God's will? I suspect it pleases God when we treat ourselves tenderly, as if we are all sacred.

I am a buttercup

In memory of mom,
Inger Marit, 1929-2000

I am a buttercup. I am a delicate.
A spring from earth and heaven above,
I am fragility itself; I am love.

Treat me tenderly, that I may be
all that I am intended to be,
happy, joyous and free.

I am a delicate spring from life.
Do not trample upon me
thy will, thy judgments, thy expectations,
thy way of life.

Please, instead, look upon me
and raise within me a shining,
as I bear witness to a beauty
alighting from thine eyes.

I am a buttercup. I am fragility itself.
You let me be...help me be...
a delicate spring from life,
a buttercup intended to be me.

Loving you tenderly always, Randi   73

TWO

A Philosopher's Dilemma

With a sense of disconnection from self, others and God almost complete, we may begin to entertain the plausibility of various philosophical viewpoints. However, when we live from the neck up, we begin a process of mind twisting dilemmas. Ultimately, we may become mentally shipwrecked and engage in laughter at ourselves. Notable philosophers such as Descartes, Plato, Socrates, Sartre, Kant, Aquinas and Hegel, to name a few, have also attempted to overcome obstacles in grasping 'truth.'

They openly call everything into doubt and attempt to unearth their deepest biases. They attempt to define the indefinable and they arrive at various opinions on issues of God and immortality. After I entertain the plausibility of various philosophical viewpoints, it seems preferable to undertake the onerous task of judging what my 'truth' is. It seems wrong to blindly accept truth based on the authority of others and to blame the consequences of my life on the wisdom of others, or on the so-called will of God.

For example, Descartes arrived at a mind boggling proposition when he concluded, "I think, therefore I am!" Yet, because Descartes laid the foundation for contemporary mathematics, he also paved the way for both church and science allowing theologians to further study humans having finite or everlasting lives, and for scientists to further study mass and energy.

Plato suggests that "the unexamined life is not worth living." The famous Socratic method of teaching appears to be "to teach humility and arouse curiosity." Aristotle was an empiricist, anchoring all knowledge of reality in perceptual experience.

A self-proclaimed atheist, Sartre has said of God, "Failing to take root in my heart, [God] vegetated in me for awhile, then He died." However, in 1958, at age 53, Sartre participated in a protest against the Algerian War and in a press conference on human rights. This suggests that regardless of whether we personally accept that there is a God, or not, or whether we have a deep and personal relationship with a very loving and good God, or not, Sartre's and humankind's true merit and virtue will be found in our choices that reflect our value for human life.

Kant declared that only two things inspire genuine awe, "the starry sky above and the moral law within. Good will is intrinsically good; its value is wholly self-contained and utterly independent of its external relations…it does not depend even on the results it manages to produce as the consequences of human action. The ultimate principle of morality must be a moral law that is capable of guiding us to the right action in application to every possible set of circumstances." Kant seems to suggest that we have a responsibility to act in goodwill and to detach from outcomes because we can place complete reliance on this guiding principle. I suggest Kant's ultimate guiding principle of morality is in modern times otherwise known as intuition.

Kant says that "moral obligation is the notion that right actions are those that practical reason would will as universal law." I suggest, an individual can access and be divinely guided by this inspiring universal moral law when we connect with God. When we rely on human ingenuity alone, we place reliance on our limitations.

The Sunlight of Absolute Spirit works through people willing to be channels of helpfulness, love and goodwill.

When we invite into our hearts and mind this spirit of goodwill, we allow for the opportunity of being intuitively guided to bring right action into every possible set of circumstances.

We trust in this proper alignment of our will working in responsive cooperation with God's will, whether we understand the practical reasons for it, or not.

Paying attention to how we are helped when we surrender to love, we come to believe in a power greater than ourselves; we end the illusion of separation and our focus shifts from self to others.

Kant seems to suggest that we will know what good will is when our sense of duty overcomes our evident self-interest and obvious desire to do otherwise, and that acting on duty is an expression of our reverence for the necessity of the universality of this moral law. God's will is the universal moral law within that seeks to care, nourish and protect life. Therefore, humankind's first duty belongs to the protection and care of our planet, our own lives and peace between its inhabitants, regardless of our self interests. When we embrace love, cherish and value our own life, our moral duty to protect and care for others and our planet becomes clear. The decision to value life, all life, will overcome our evident self interest to do otherwise.

Many of us believe that it seems God does not exist, because if God is defined as meaning infinite goodness there would be no evil, no tsunami's, in the world. Therefore, God cannot exist. Therein, we disconnect from God when we experience misery and death, and blame our unhappy consequences on God.

For example, we all experience 'emotional tsunami's' in life. My mother died a painful death and my sister, a non-believer, said with some disgust, "And just where is your all loving and merciful God, now?" But, how is it possible to feel anger toward a God we disbelieve? God does not bring hardship and misery into our lives, we do. Even during times of emotional tsunamis and other natural disasters, God's love is present through an outpouring of human actions willing to bring aide and comfort. We help the helpless. Love is always outward flowing, with no expectations attached to the giving.

Regarding my mother's death, the presence of God's compassion and kindness is found in our ability to bring comfort and care to her and to each other. God works through people willing to be a channel of helpfulness, love and goodwill. Therefore, when Augustine says (Enchiridion xi): "Since God is the highest good, [God] would not allow any evil to exist in [God's] works, unless [God's] omnipotence and goodness were such as to bring good even out of evil." We need not understand God's will, only accept and be grateful for the good that is, was and will be. When we look for the good, we find it; we grow, become grateful for all and accepting of what is. We trust in God.

Therefore, the infinite goodness and positive flow of energy that originates and emanates from an all knowing and loving God, is that God does allow evil to exist and out of it produce good. It is only in the duality of our thinking that we judge 'good' and 'bad.' The good that comes from evil, may simply involve making choices that honors rather than destroys life, starting with our own. We are responsible for the outcome of our ego- or spiritual-driven choices. Therefore, the existence of choosing either good or evil action rests within the conscience of every individual comprising the whole of humankind.

We may conclude that we are ultimately required to make only one decision in life: To choose life, or to choose death, knowing these choices present themselves to us in every way, every day. We are all aware of the ravages of war and its toll on human life. When we acknowledge the gruesome impact this 'global inner-terrorist' has left in mankind's wake, the good that can come from evil atrocities is to simply choose anew. We may ask ourselves, "What could I have done differently? Why didn't I?" Ask and sense what comes...the truth may surprise and reveal our deepest fear of all; it is to be vulnerable in our need for each other. The blood of all our soldiers need be spilled for not; we may choose life and help each other in a host of cooperative ventures.

Note: Evil spelled backwards is Live. Therefore, to choose to 'live' is to step away from its opposite. To destroy life is 'evil.' Therefore, the only decision we need to make is to consciously choose life. We can embrace, cherish and live with deep human satisfaction. As written before, two masters we cannot both serve and survive. We must pick one and commit.

In any event, Hegel also offers his opinions, i.e., "a metaphysico-religious view of "Absolute Spirit" which draws on...the identity of the universe and God, together with theistic ideas concerning the necessary "self-consciousness" of God...Hegel's view...is [that] as bearers of this developing self-consciousness of God [we] are those finitely-embodied inhabitants of the universe – we humans – can [also] be..."finite-infinites."

Therefore, we can consciously choose to be God's bearers of peace by developing this same said self consciousness, self awareness, in cooperation with God's will. For the benefit of our self and others, we may connect with our universal moral law that exists within. When we pay attention to intuition, we can make a commitment to follow its guidance at every moment.

Even as a young child, I possessed a natural curiosity and sense of sheer wonder for life, and I enjoyed pondering philisophical questions concerning the big picutre. For example, "Why am I here? Who am I? What's it all about Alphie and Omega?" Such as Descartes, "I think." As Plato, "I examine my life." As Socrates, I seek to, "teach humility and arouse curiosity." As Sartre, "I am atheist when I disconnect from God, but remain a humanitarian." As Kant, I believe "Good will is intrinsically good," and I accept the necessity to let go and trust in the outcome as having the possibility of being far more desirous than anything I could create by reliance on my own ingenuity. As Aquinas, "God does allow for good to come even out of evil." And, as Hegel, "it is connection with self and our conscience that is linked with "Absolute Spirit."

Truth is what truth is, as it exists within the eye of the beholder. The creative human being answers only to the calling of our individuality. We must not seek truth until we are willing to have truth lift us from our limited reality and catapult our destiny into a sphere of wholeness. This experience will forever smash the illusion that we exist separate and apart. Yes, we must not rest on the laurels of reason, rather we must nurture our greater instinct for survival, intuitive guidance. When we think outside of the box and lift from self, we become one with the grand prism of light and our divine spark within. Be prepared for a full flight to freedom, and become entirely unravelled as the truth sets us free to be true to ourselves. Live truth, beauty and joy; we are beauties within the eye of our beholder.

We can never absolutely know the truth of who we are and why we are here, so let the laughter of the gods thunder. It amuses me to realize that, "Man cannot create a single flea, yet he creates 'gods' by the dozen" (Montaigne). Regardless of the opinions of histories most notable philosophic thinkers, various religious doctrines and the heartfelt bias of romantic humanists, in humility I suggest that any opinion is like memory. The thoughts that create opinion and memory are;

1. similarly fired by accidentals and celled in superstitiously arranged supposition, i.e., a random copulation of thoughts and emotions that spark throughout the stratums of our unique genetic composition and all derived from restricted and sometimes deceitful sense perceptions,

2. distorted by time, deeply rooted biases and insecurities,

3. pickled in emotion, and

4. concluded in illusion: The starting points of our thoughts that form both opinion and memory are as

illusive as their respective conversational endings; this is no discernible beginning or ending at all.

Therefore, memory and opinion are as mysterious as the ideas of monotheism, soul immortality and ad-infinitum universes.

My personal dilemma seems to be preoccupied with the conflict between pre-determination and self-determination; God's will and our will. What appears to be in need of reconciliation are our egotistical self-contained minds and our infinite self in connection with the mysterious agent that encompasses all energy. Perhaps there is no conflict at all; it is the gift of purposeful belonging and to know harmony with our destiny.

This leads to the problem of discerning whose life is it, and in understanding how the mysterious forces of the individual and collective human connections (God consciousness) operate in cooperation for the benefit of all. This dilemma only becomes reconciled when we accept that our lives are not just about us, but that we belong to the whole of humankind. Whether we like it, or not, we form part of the whole — we belong.

From that comes the knowledge of personal responsibility and that if willing, we can all contribute to the positive outcome of the whole—peace on earth and goodwill toward all. This dilemma is further resolved when we accept that we can no more use reason to find God, as we can use reason to dismiss the idea of God. We may certainly try to support an argument either way as many philosophers have, but none are cast in stone as absolute truths.

Further, since our thoughts are inextricably connected to all, it is possible that intuition is our personal guide that connects with a universal moral law. We need only ask for contact with that guiding principle to occur and be willing to receive the intuitive insight that follows. It's just that simple, irrespective of where this comes from. However, we must always be willing to accept responsibility for the quality of our thoughts, actions and resulting outcomes.

We can arrest the devil, our inner terrorist (the evil temptress to our anger, fears and insecurities that rob us of life). We can ask for God's help and say, "Ah, I see you Fear. I release you to the light and replace you with love; we can take a leap for life. We can acknowledge and release debilitating emotions, purify and cleanse ourselves; we can trust in the light of our own life.

> *Seen or not seen, spoken or not spoken, thoughts have power. They influence everything around us, particularly our own well being. Thoughts have the power to alter energy and can travel through time and space in no time at all.*
>
> *The good news is we have the power to be the stop watch of our own thoughts and at the same time be of intrinsic and infinite value to God's harmonious clock work of the universe.*

We can choose to think positive, or to think negative. We can choose to be grateful, or to whine in self pity. We can choose to become givers, rather than takers. We can choose to serve only one master. When we choose only to exist in a state of acceptance, trust and gratitude, everything we can change, will change and become harmonious.

Questioning how the combination of both reason and intuition function in connection with self and the collective human consciousness becomes moot. As does the question, "Does life as we know it exist in self-perpetuating chaos, or in a state of self-perpetuating ordered flux?" While philosophers and scientists may continue to be compelled to entertain these thoughts, our bottom line will depend entirely on our willingness to connect with a force that helps us harmonize with its kindness, because that will dictate our actions and how we treat our self and each other while we are alive.

The truths that continually resurface throughout history are that there is a God and of ourselves alone we are not it. We form part of life's infinite expressions of creation. For all our truth seeking, it is possible that the most intellectually articulated minds are confined within the similar constraints of all human minds. Philosophers and scientists alike continually hit a similarly developed cranium wall of logic, wherein they have entertained the multiplicity of truth possibilities within the vigorous dialogue of their self-examined minds. This has led to frustrated madness and states of inconsolable depression. When we rely on reason alone we are prone to superiority, which is non-conducive to creating peace within ourselves, or our nations. We can close our eyes and know all hearts beat the same, break and cry the same.

Despite exhaustive efforts, what remains is that we are born, and we die. Our bodies have a destiny, and only the when and how remains a mystery. Our minds are not just along for the ride, hardly-har. Our minds are mutable and transformable. When we allow our mind to surrender and accept that our best thinking on its own rarely produces the best result, we open a gateway and begin to access the creative heaven within; we become co-creators with our highest good.

Should we become willing to live, we must necessarily catapult downwards and begin a process of integration with our hearts. When we achieve fluidity, we expose an opportunity to be guided by a universal moral law and we can live harmoniously. Together with brothers and sisters worldwide the destiny of humankind can be transformed while we yet live.

Nevertheless, it appears that for any given opinion there is reflected in polarized opposition another opinion. At the round table, that's what great debaters enjoy. Whether there is concern for peaceful resolution, truth, or not, debates can become all about being most right and winning. Therefore, when we rely solely on the use of reason, the genius of self-contained thoughts, polarized opinions can be debated with equal strength and merit. What often results is the shipwrecking of both and synthesis into an ever enlarging mass of murk. What is true, virtuous and right action can become lost in mental debris. However, when we come together united in a commitment to access a similarly understood harmonious genius, whose only motivation is peace and goodwill, miracle-making begins. 89

On the rare occasion when we experience eureka gut thrills, and think we have triumphed over the muck and mire of our own mental quicksand, it is then that we may engage in laughter at ourselves. We remain uncertain whether we've experienced a stroke of genius, or a silly joke! Therefore, opinion and memory can appear to be;

a) all mirrors,

b) fragments of multi-coloured smoke screens. Truth remains ever illusive, or does it?

Entertaining the plausibility of various philosophical viewpoints begins a process of mind twisting dilemmas. While the laughter of the gods may thunder, we may invite ourselves to do cartwheels through the rain instead of thumb sucking beneath a table of unworthy authority and influences of custom and popular prejudice. From one mysterious pineal gland to another, I suggest that we hug ourselves, each other and literally lighten up! Such as shifting sand, my position has evolved from the famous 'thinking man's' to that of a yogi trying to unknot itself.

Perhaps it has occurred to everyone but this late bloomer, that I must accept the illusiveness of 'truth' and my inherent mind limitations. I must accept these limitations as

God's protective myelin sheath; perhaps it protects me from myself. While I believe that our lives are pre-determined, it might as well not be because we self-determine that pre-determination every moment that we think, feel, intuit and live — so active participants we must remain.

In the final analysis, it need not concern us whether we can ever rationalize the beauty of creation. All that is required for us to live a life of serenity simply rests in our acceptance and enjoyment of the bountiful blessings of what is. When we trust that everything is perfectly placed for purposes promising our greatest benefit, we can have the courage to connect with the truth of our own reality, and commit every day to doing our part in changing what we can. When we see the truth of our own reality in a light of positive attitudes, we become part of the beauty of creation and know peace with self and others.

Perhaps there is nothing illusive about truth and beauty at all. Perhaps truth and beauty is starring us in the face, and only when our eyes open will we know truth and beauty is found in a newborns first gasp of air. And as a maturing soul, we will know truth, beauty and love is found when we release our final sigh.

While philosophers undertake to define the indefinable, as harnessed thinkers, I believe the synoptic yoke is on us all, and for good reason. We can't handle the truth until we become willing to live the truth. When we abandon our propensity to live from the neck up and surrender to a process of integration between our hearts and minds, it becomes possible to connect with love and breath; we become centered with Spirit. When we connect with self, others and God, we may begin to live Truth and know "…behold, the kingdom of God is within you" (Luk 17:21).

When we know God is within, we begin to experience the presence of 'grace in action' at every moment we choose to wake up, take notice and unite as a team. Agreeing that our lives are predestined, whether we were in priori agreement with a Creator or not, we can know that in every particular set of circumstances we are called to respond by consciously choosing to act with a spirit of goodwill. Answering the call of this moral law within is our free choice. To make our destiny worthy of remembering requires spiritual willingness, emotional commitment and mental discipline. Its reward of 'grace in action' results when our hearts and minds cooperate in unity and alignment with life's spirit of goodwill.

However, even though we come to believe in a responsive God who loves us, there is often one more event that challenges faith and has the power to finish us off. If we succumb to the urgings of our inner-terrorist, give up on life and begin to self destruct, we collapse into the field of the faithless and we are the lost and bewildered ones. When we reclaim and value our own life, and all life, we gratefully acknowledge, "It breathes us." It comforts us to know we need never feel alone. Isolation is a choice. When we surrender again, deeper and deeper into the presence of love, we arrest this urge in favour of life. We can rise once more and become wiser, more loving and resilient than before; we grow.

I often wake up in the middle of the night, with right palm firmly placed on my forehead and left hand out-stretched toward the heavens, proclaiming rather loudly, "I know nothing!" Wanting to see...not wanting to see...I remain humble and open. Trust in the process; together we can continue to reach, grow, awaken and rest in thankful contemplation; we can allow for more and more beauty to unfold within the truth of our own hearts.

Resting
in thankful
contemplation,
we see the beauty
that is found
in the truth
of our own
reality.

~ Randi Done

Albert Einstein

*All religions, arts and sciences are branches of the
same tree.
All these aspirations are directed toward ennobling
[humankind's] life,
Lifting it from the sphere of mere physical
existence,
and leading the individual
towards freedom.*

AND

*Through the release of atomic energy, our
generation has brought into the world
the most revolutionary force since prehistoric man's
discovery of fire.
This basic force of the universe cannot be fitted into
the outmoded concept
of narrow nationalisms.*

—Albert Einstein

THREE

COLLAPSING & RE-BIRTHING

Converging into the most glorious re-birthing time frame of our lives, no words suffice to convey the love David and I shared. Symbolic of resplendent zest, hope and faith in humanity we lay in wild fields of daisies filled with thankful hearts. Hiking high above the clouds we scanned the necessity for peaceful connections in the valley below and beyond. Naked, we swam to healing restoration in pristine lakes, rejoicing in superior powers of goodness, rightness and light. Coupling in luminosity, people stopped in their tracks. Awestruck, they gawked in wonder, jealousy and suspicious judgment. Nothing could collapse us.   99

When David scooped me up into his huge arms, we could never be certain where I began and he ended. Circling in joy we chorused, "You are the love of my life, the heart and soul of my life; I'll spend the rest of my life just loving you." Our eternal connection together seemed to have less to do with our human pleasures and more to do with fulfilling some higher purpose. We planned to improve God's world by partnering in the creation of healthy hearts and global communities. The two of us desired only to give back to the world the secret of blessing the self without fear, anger, sorrow or shame. There was a benevolent God after all. Nothing could collapse us.

Sliced by trauma, I remember the day destiny changed. I knew something was wrong. David looked ashen. Choked by unforgiving grief, I prayed my guts out trying to save him — to breathe life into him. Courageously clinging to every ounce of energy to stay, his parting words promised, "All is not lost. Our time will come. It must!" Yet, there was something greater than the will of our souls playing dice with our lives. On our wedding day, releasing his final sigh, David died.

Falling into a time frame heaped in despair, I felt as if an ax split us apart severing our universe of equilibrium.

Like a collapsed tree that rots from the inside and becomes petrified in time, I became a weight of reality that froze in eternity. Rocking back and forth pounding my fists on the floor, I clutched at my body in futility, screaming, "Why God? Why?"

I felt like a Barbie doll, twisted and mangled by the will of God. As if entering W.W. III, the bombardments within my mind were relentless. My AK-47 was fully armed with righteousness, firing in rage at everything and everyone. Charged with fear, self pity and contempt I rapidly engaged in personal genocide. Circling in madness, I became a rat on a treadmill running as fast as I could getting nowhere in great haste. There could be no life worth living after David. Lacking wisdom, my godless thoughts were intent on maneuvering my future into one predictable possibility — death.

The black clouds were rolling in without egalitarian diffusion. Failing to listen, I willfully blocked thunder warnings chorusing, "Glory, glory, hallelujah! The saints come marching on, and on...But, the ants go marching two by two. And you will all go marching down to your graves...Get out...of the dug out...Boom! Boom! Boom! Now!"

Because I held a perception of God and value for David's life in equally high regard, I'm uncertain which loss was greater. Strangely, a formal feeling of resignation came. That was the day I closed the curtain on the idea of a good God. Lost and bewildered, I engaged in a philosophical diatribe on God's benevolence, or lack thereof. I proffered,

> There is no God: Certainly not a benevolent God, or an evil genius. God conquers nothing: Certainly not life and certainly not death. If there is a God, It is an indifferent God. God reveals itself to me as being nothing more than the existence of ad-infinitum collapsing and re-birthing, within different specific time frames, in spaces incomprehensible. This process exists not only for our secular selves, but for all the stars and gods in the multiplicity of universes yet unknown, or unborn. It is motion encased in a series of seemingly perverse conversions and convulsions, without beginning or ending. It just is…the Alpha and the Omega.

There is no accounting for the seemingly random accidentals that hallmark our lives into chunks of joy, despair and resignation. In clenched frustration, I continued lamenting, "Oh, God! David! I miss you!" As if I was a violet fragment encased within a translucent rainbow, I thought I heard echoing back, "I'm with you always!" Something of my spirit began drifting skyward, forever attaching itself to the Star of David.

Knowing the chain may lengthen, but it never breaks, I continued with, "God speed my love home to me. Roll the dice one more time. Spin out only those heavenly sevens. Shield me from those despairing snake eyes. Oh God...Can you hear my cry?" Heard, or not heard, I felt compelled to release my suffering, or die. Crumpling to my knees in desperation, I prayed, "God, please help me!" Surrendering to the place where stillness reigns, my faintest light flickered.

AWAKENING

As if awakening from the big sleep,
resonating within my deepest parts
was a pulse for life made greater in its need.
Yet I wondered, "Where is love?"

And so it was that I went in search of God,
Only to discover a multiplicity of faiths,
Only to collapse into humility,
Only to discover within,
A multi-faceted jewel,
Like a diamond,
Iridescent,
Reflecting,
Refracting, and
Lighting my way,
From every angle.
This goblet runneth over,
And I saw that God is very good.
Love just is~in everything and everyone.
There for the asking, and there for our giving,
We find the place from where we may begin.

~ Randi Done

"God does not play dice with our lives" (Albert Einstein). With eyes wide open, we may always choose a path brightly lit with love. Yet, I chose the long and arduous path—my way—the hard way. Returning to peace of mind, divine and loving universal mind, my focus shifted from self to others. In quiet contemplation, I became willing to live, love and nourish my own life. With grace and growing insight, I became willing to be helpful to my family—humanity.

When we awaken and surrender to love;

* *we return to peace of mind, divine and loving universal mind,*

* *we look for the good in everything and everyone, and we find it,*

* *we trust the cards we are dealt are perfectly placed for purposes promising our greatest benefit,*

* *we trust in perfect timing in all things and at all times; we trust in God, and*

• *we begin reaching toward our greater destiny, peace on earth and goodwill toward all.*

Experiencing the tragic juxtaposition of great pain with great joy, results in the necessity of balancing our huge emotional displacements. We can ask for help and empower forces within of greater life giving strength, feeling more empathic toward everyone engaged in a journey of acceptance and the courage to change. We must choose which side of the fence we are willing to exit and grow toward.

> *Knowing we are spiritual beings having human experiences, God's purpose for our existence seems to rest in our growing acceptance, compassionate understanding and value for life— all life. Abandoning malcontent, harmony is reclaimed in favour of peace, love and joy.*

Remembering Jesus said, "Suffer little children...to come to me: for such is the kingdom of Heaven" (Mat 19:14), our hostile retort may be, "Hells bells! I'd rather have a little less suffering and a little more joy, thank you very much!" Knowing that love is the solution to every set of circumstances, with wisdom we can all swim toward healing restoration by relaxing into thankful hearts; we need never feel alone.

Returning to the truth of my own reality, I stood at the shoreline allowing rhythmic waves to wash away my sorrow. Discovering above the clouds the sky is always blue, I chose to hike high above my own clouds and found faith in life shining with hope. Lighter and freer, my heart opened wide filling with sparkling joy and peace divine. And so it goes…we begin reaching and growing.

Reaching

In reaching our greater destiny,
we become more beautiful in our understanding
of what love is, and what love is not.

~Randi Dong

Love, when felt at all deeply,

is the spirit of transcendence into the divine;

we must lose ourselves to find ourselves.

Accepting the ideas that a punishing God and original sin are man-made fabrications, separation from our Creator and each other becomes an illusion. Reaching clarity and genuine humility we may request of our evolved understanding, "Guide us in loving-kindness. Mend our ways into your most perfect fashion." We may all resolve the morality of existence by embracing no other popular prejudice than making life choices our only guardian angel.

We can run, but not hide from our evolving spiritual collapsing and re-birthing. We must embrace the notion that we affect our own gradations of spiritual regress, or aggress. By burning our way through the "cherubim's, and a flaming sword [that turns] every way" (Genesis 3:24), we can miraculously survive slices of trauma, but only if we do not feign genuine affection.

To reject love is to reject life, *"and those who fear life are already three parts dead"* (Bertrand Russell: *Marriage and Morals*).

Love is the indestructible healing energy. Love is gentle; it is our soothing balm. With a life of its own, love is not created or destroyed; it is eternal.

Love is always out flowing, and love is always inclusive never exclusive. It appears as if from nowhere. Love is not always immediately recognizable, is sometimes a nuisance and often calls us from every angle.

Love comes in different pastels and each hue emits its own unique union of translucent vibrancy. Such as our Creator, love just is.

Love's highest frequency and kindest intention propels us toward our most creative, harmonious and loving potential.

Whether we cooperate by living in alignment with our Creator's intention, or not, is our free choice. This choice presents itself to us in every way, every day.

When we make a conscious decision to honour life, all life, we wake up to a universe willing to support our commitments leaving us full with gratitude.

It takes courage to live, and live fully. It takes more courage to love, surrender and love deeply and completely; it takes a leap of faith and love is faiths reward.

Stressing the importance of honest introspection, Shakespeare provides a key to honouring our own life and process of self-actualization;

This above all: to thine own self be true,

And it must follow, as the night, the day,

Thou canst not then be false to any man (Hamlet, I, iii).

With awareness of our debilitating emotions we can play the game of catch and release. "Ah," we may say, "I see you and I let you go. You no longer serve a useful purpose. I replace you with clarity." Removing denial from every aspect of our life, honesty with self and others sets us free to be true to our self. We can look in the mirror and like what we see. Allowing our faintest light to flicker we will know what our next best step is. With integrity we will be guided to do our part in life's master plan.

David and I have played our part. My next best step is connecting with spirit, breathing deeply and completely as one golden beam. Although preferring to marry and become pregnant with the life of David, it was our destiny to part in sacrifice. For what purpose we need not understand; only accept and trust. Perhaps in God's loving wisdom David's life was released from mine that we may both grow and shine.

We can welcome forgiving and compassionate love toward self and others.

We can know we are all the sons and daughters of one Creator.

Firmly rooted in unity, we can renew ourselves as evolved trees of life and become the apples of our Creator's eye.

We can offer ourselves and say, "Take the apple back and show us your way."

By embarking upon a co-created future, we can resurrect self and humanity.

Lifted, we can shift toward wholeness and become all that we are intended—responsible and free.

Clinging to the popular prejudice of praising God and blaming the devil, we negate personal responsibility over all our individual and collective actions. By releasing the existence of duality, we have at once found our self and the essence of loving connection with our Creator. Since we mysteriously affect and are affected by our collective energy, we can miraculously resurrect humanity as cooperative rays of light. We can responsibly co-create a new reality by adjusting the quality of our thoughts and actions.

The imperative necessity to fuse in forgiveness has arrived. By relying on the living presence of sacred grace within, we can ask and be open to knowing how loving-kindness might guide us. When we become willing to look for the good, we awaken to a process of finding the blessing in everything and everyone. Discovering our greatest blessings are spurred by our most difficult circumstances, we see the beauty that is found in the truth of our own reality. Resurrected from misery, we are then able to offer hope and be helpful to others suffering a similar plight.

When we begin with prayer and quiet contemplation, we will witness the unfolding of ideals that result from inner guidance and courageous action. This ideological tsunami will cleanse our broken hearts and global communities, and convulse humanity into a dynamic and expanding spiritual territory. We will thereby heal the way to new beginnings intent on empowering the throes of a common good. Reaching our greater destiny, we will know peace on earth and goodwill toward humankind.

Since the life process will conquer our arrogance we must release our suffering by honouring life, all life, with the clarity of loving-kindness. We must put our AK-47's aside, avoiding W.W. III and all forms of planetary genocide. We must return to the place where stillness reigns and maneuver our future into predictable possibilities of peaceful connections in the valley below and far beyond.

> *Surrendering to love, we return to the place where stillness reigns.*
>
> *Together we can light a torch of hope for humanity and remember the day destiny changed.*
>
> *While life has an evolutionary will of its own, we are all colourful threads that interweave in the quilting of God's overall fabric of flux and glorious design.*
>
> *We form part of God's infinite expressions of beauty and joy.*

As for myself, I'm taking this goblet to Greece where I shall break bread and drink the reddest of wines. With resplendent zest I shall smash plates, dance on tables and swish my skirt high. I shall become like a wild thing that makes my heart sing, collapsing into the most glorious re-birthing time frame of my life. Patron onlookers will gawk in shock, wonder and pride. Others will raise eyebrows of jealousy and suspicious judgment. Let them gawk. I'm not in love with suffering and self persecution. Neither shall I cower behind bullish enmity, sorrow or shame.

Nourishing self and our baby universe, we can feel safe in knowing our moral enlightenment is unfolding precisely on schedule.

Therefore, with a dare the devil wink and a crystal clink, I enjoin, "Chin up! Can you come out to frolic today? Celebrate the cyclical solstices of life, especially our darkest moments. Our sun only appears to have paused before returning in ecliptic resplendence. Come, love life beneath constellations of endless collapsing and re-birthing! No doubt, such as on the seventh day, our Creator continues to rest in satisfaction and sustain itself in gamma ray equilibrium, placing the clarity of loving-kindness firmly within our beating hearts. "

Thankful

Resting
in thankful
contemplation
we see the beauty
that is found
in the truth
of our own
hearts.
Forming part of
our eternal All,
we see...
It matters
not the most
the amount of time
we have on earth;
It matters most
the love we share
that marks its lasting worth.
Forming part of our eternal All,
we see our part and more...
Resting and reaching,
the stars of our greater destiny,
we are made most glorious
in our understanding of
what love is, and what love is not.
Resting
in thankful
contemplation
we see clearly,
Truth...Beauty...Love,
raising within us a sharing
alighting our eternal All.

~Randi Done

John F. Kennedy
US President

Few will have the greatness to bend history itself,
but each of us can work to change a small portion of events,
and in the total of all those sets
will be written the history of this generation.

And

"But peace does not rest in the charters and covenants alone. It lies in the hearts and minds of all people. So let us not rest all our hopes on parchment and on paper, let us strive to build peace, a desire for peace, a willingness to work for peace in the hearts and minds of all of our people. I believe that we can. I believe the problems of human destiny are not beyond the reach of human beings."

—John F. Kennedy, US President

FOUR

THE GLASS

MENAGERIE
An Interpretation

In his libertine creation of <u>The Glass Menagerie</u>, Tennessee Williams presents several ideas at once. It is his underlying current of hope that his readers understand, "that the future becomes the present, the present the past, and the past turns into everlasting regret if you don't plan for it" (<u>Angles of Vision</u>, 4,1193). Williams emphasizes the complex interaction between reality and memory, and shows how this framework sets the cast for our current perceptual stage. It is this interaction that allows us the opportunity of continuously re-shaping a revolving economy and political ideology, while simultaneously being shaped by society's influences. I will also suggest how our memory of JFK's political ideals can be a reminder of hope for humanity.

It is when we are feeling pain that we are presented with an opportunity to question our current perceptual stage. Pursuing our own happiness requires courage to bust through illusions, and to entertain new possibilities in the continuous election of life. Therefore, we must challenge those beliefs that contribute to our current stage of unhappiness. If we refuse to actively engage in the positive construction of our own destiny, in the present, the logical consequence will be the perpetuation of faulty thinking that contributes to our own illusions and less than satisfying reality. Until we open our eyes and become aware of the truth of our own reality, we will remain in a stage where we continue to repeat the same lines, and to make similar choices that result in similar unhappy outcomes.

We are, therefore, called to choose between creativity and stagnation, and the alternatives of integrity, or destruction and despair. In his melancholic plea, Tennessee Williams hopes to extinguish "the slow implacable fires of human desperation" (1,1178) by offering "the enslaved section of [middle class] American society" (1,1178) his "truth in the pleasant disguise of illusion" (1, 1179). He asks us to purge our superficial and erroneously superior way of perceiving our self and our place in the world and to please stop "matriculating in a school for the blind" (1,1179).

As evidenced by Tom, "time is the longest distance between two places," (7,1222) which in memory is no distance at all. His memory was queued by a "familiar bit of music" (7, 1222), ten years following the economic decay of the mid-30s and his departure from his family. Tom's motivation to leave his mother and sister had less to do with his desire for adventure than it had to do with his desire to escape from his mother's domineering superiority, her incessant "interruption of his creative labour," (3,1187) and her expectation that Tom should assume her husband's role in taking care of the family's 'plans and provisions.'

Tom was "fired for writing a poem on the lid of a shoe box" (7,1222). Had he embraced the ideal "To thine own self be true" (Hamlet I, iii), such as Shakespeare and JFK, Tom would have been similarly motivated by the powers of creativity and personal integrity. He would not have come to feel like "dead leaves that were brightly coloured but torn away from the branches" (7, 1222). He may, such as Shakespeare, have come to experience prosperity as did the rising middle class of the sixteenth century.   123

As a touch of dramatic irony, Tom came to realize with the onslaught of W.W.II that he was mistaken when he said, "Yes, until there's war. That's when adventure becomes available to the masses!" (6, 1206). Since "memory is seated predominantly in the heart," (1,1178) Tom's feeling of guilt for leaving Laura was undoubtedly "magnified thousands of times by imagination" (7,1215). Tom's eyes had failed him, or he had failed his eyes. From this micro-perspective, Tom's no longer workable perceptual stage elected to vote in favor of stagnation and the alternatives of personal destruction and despair.

From a macro-perspective, Jim symbolizes the political ideology of Capitalism and how touting the party line has influenced revolving economies from the sixteenth- to twentieth-centuries. In his theory of political evolution, i.e., the change from Capitalism to Communism, Marx did not foresee the rise of unions. Socialism was a mere transitional phase between the two. Yet, "There were disturbances of labor, sometimes pretty violent" (1, 1179). Despite mere tinges of an emerging social consciousness, competitive Capitalism continues to thrive rather than cooperative ventures. Members of the huge middle class of America, such as the Wingfield family, unthinkingly "function as one interfused mass of automatism" (1, 1178).

Jim "seemed always at the point of defeating the law of gravity...you would logically expect him to arrive at nothing short of the White House by the time he was thirty" (6,1200). Jim is ambitious and obsessed with his own sense of greatness. "Well, well, well, well—look how big my shadow is when I stretch!" (7, 1216). And, "Sure. I'm Superman!" (7, 1210). "He had tremendous Irish good nature and vitality with the scrubbed and polished look of white chinaware" (6,1200). He says, "I believe in the future of television!" (7,1215). The way election campaigns appear to be won and lost in the media nowadays, perhaps Jim will become the first and only Irish Catholic President of the United States of America.

Is it possible that Tennessee Williams could be referring to the politically idealistic and upwardly mobile JFK, even though The Glass Menagerie was written in 1944? Coincidentally, in 1943 at age 29, Kennedy received the Purple Heart for rescuing fellow sailors in the South Pacific during W.W.II. JFK began his way to The White House and the U.S.A. presidency. Furthermore, it is likely that his tremendously good Irish looks were something the electoral campaign did capitalize. Does Williams model his character called Jim after John F. Kennedy, disguised in the pleasant balm of illusion?

Williams refers to Jim as "being an emissary from a world of reality that [the Wingfield's, i.e., locusts] were somehow set apart from" (1, 1179). He said, "I'm going to sell you a bill of goods!" (6, 1205). His underhanded mission seems to consist of conveying several odious beliefs:

1. His prejudices, "Oh, that kraut-head!" (7, 1214). W.W.II started when Germany invaded Poland on September 1, 1939.

2. His value for huge corporations, "Think of the fortune made by the guy that invented the first piece of chewing gum. Amazing, huh? (7, 1211). Yet, JFK having negotiated a deal to maintain current steel prices, when they increased their prices he accused the companies of "a wholly unjustifiable and irresponsible defiance of the public trust."

3. His value for the "Century of Progress…what impressed me most was the Hall of Science" (7, 1211). The Space Race was one of the major events included in Kennedy's presidency.

There is a tendency, if allowed to be perceived unchecked, to see and hear what we want, or expect to see and hear.

Jim O'Connor (Oh, con her) said to Laura, "I could put on an act for you, Laura, and say lots of things without being very sincere. But this time I am," (7, 1218). Williams implies that most of the time Jim is an ambitious manipulator, selfish and prideful in the extreme.

Regardless, "the sky falls" (7, 1220) for both Laura and Amanda with the news of Jim's pending marriage to Betty. "The holy candles of Laura's face have been snuffed out. There is a look of almost infinite desolation" (7, 1219). As long as Laura continues to manufacture illusions and Amanda is obsessed with "Ou sont les neiges" (1, 1182), i.e., her family's former status, they will continue to repeat the same mistakes. Amanda and Laura both cast a spoiled ballot in the election of their lives.

Are we being misled by Tennessee Williams' sarcasm when he writes that Jim "is the long delayed but always expected something that we live for" (1, 1179)? Is Williams suggesting that only if we have eyes to see can we recognize that the trick is that Jim, an apparent symbol of integrity upon whom we can rely and trust, is an untrustworthy, reckless, albeit charming skirt-chaser? Is Jim a wolf in sheep's clothing? Or, keeping our eyes wide open, is Williams suggesting that although imperfect, Jim is our hope for the future?

Laura's glass menagerie is symbolic of the fragility of human relationships and of the planet. "Glass breaks so easily," (7, 1217) and "is something you have to take good care of" (7, 1215). The unicorn is a heraldic proclamation of the approach of something imminent—possible extinction of Amanda and Laura's current perceptual stage, or of the planet. Tennessee Williams appears to have future visionary and political forecasting abilities by suspecting the onslaught of disastrous events.

Despite John F. Kennedy's involvement in the early developments of the Vietnam War, the Bay of Pigs invasion and the Cuban Missile Crisis, Kennedy worried about the possibility of nuclear war and the fragility of our entire planet. Was it because of JFK's cool head, wisdom and guidance that all manner of untold human miseries were averted during these difficult and highly combustible political situations?

Williams writes, "for nowadays the world is lit by lightning" (7, 1222). "All the world was waiting for bombardments!" (5, 1195). "In Spain there was Guernica," (1, 1179) and what followed was our experience with the peak of "science-technology" (1, 1179), with the creation and dropping of the atom bomb on Nagasaki and Hiroshima.

Perhaps in Tennessee Williams' sarcastic melancholia he sees reality more clearly than the masses do. Williams drives home a powerful message for those who refuse to have their eyes fail them. He seems to implore his audience to consider from both a micro- and macro-perspective, "So what are we going to do for the rest of our lives?" (2, 1184). "What right [does anyone] have to jeopardize us all?" (3, 1188). "It frightens me terribly how [we] just drift along" (4,1193). How many more innocent people must die, who look like the "handsome young man in a doughboy's First World War cap," (1,1178) before we learn from our past mistakes?

The pursuit of prideful superiority over others has effectively permeated societies' memories and actions for thousands of years. Yet, we continue to war and to suffer for the same underlying reasons. By remaining trapped within self-centered perceptions of grandiosity, we blindly remain in a stage that has no alternative but to perpetuate the same outcomes. War. All such life negating beliefs and actions must be eradicated, or we shall surely become "like bits of a shattered rainbow" (7, 1222). Yet, to change ourselves may be too frightening for our global voters to even contemplate, let alone to begin participating in the process of first creating personal peace.   129

We may prefer to view Tennessee Williams as "an oddly fashioned dog who trots across [our] path at some distance" (6, 1200). Having become imbued with his somewhat dialectic melancholia, I suggest that to remain as we are, we remain as dogs who are in circles still chasing our own 'tale.' "There's such a high price for negligence in this world!" (7,1209). Humankind's habituation to war will be eradicated when we finally understand that when we create peace within ourselves, peace on our planet is not only possible, it is already on its way.

In writing The Glass Menagerie, Tennessee Williams accomplishes his objectives by emphasizing the importance of thinking about whether, or not, we have had enough pain. He poses the question, "What are we going to do for the rest of our lives?" Williams suggests that when we bust through our illusions and see the truth of our own reality we can create happy outcomes; we can answer the call from our moral law within.

It is possible within the complex interaction between reality and memory that we can all reconnect to the memory and ideals of President John F. Kennedy, and carry on his legacy of peace in action. Today, motivated to live as a friend among friends, we can all consciously commit to creating this new reality in the 21st century, for the benefit of humankind and for all our children's sake.

In conclusion, Albert Einstein suggests, "A human being is part of the whole called by us universe, a part limited in time and space. We experience ourselves, our thoughts and feelings as something separate from the rest, a kind of optical delusion of consciousness. This delusion is a kind of prison for us, restricting us to our personal desires and to affection for a few persons nearest to us. Our task must be to be free ourselves from the prison by widening our circle of compassion to embrace all living creatures and the whole of nature in its beauty...The true value of a human being is determined primarily by the measure and the sense in which they have obtained liberation from the self...We shall require a substantially new manner of thinking if humanity is to survive" (Albert Einstein, 1954).

The World is an Orchestra

The world is an orchestra and we are instruments
of a power greater than ourselves.

We must create new musical scores
intent on channeling our energies
into healing bands of harmonious longevity
and deep human satisfaction.

—Randi Done

FIVE

REIGNITING OUR TORCH OF HOPE

There are few of us living on this planet who does not remember the precise moment we heard President Kennedy was assassinated. Born May 29, 1917, at age 46 his time had stopped. Gandhi, also shot to death, "fell to the ground and the time-piece broke: it had lost its raison d'etre...and the man who had stood watch on the unfolding of the nation had descended into the bowels of the past" (Int.1). Both

Gandhi's teachings and President Kennedy's leadership are the gems that can be found in the beauty of our own past. By failing to follow in their paths, we may wonder if our own watch has stopped, or if we are just running out of time?

In 1963, even though I was only seven-years-old when President Kennedy was snuffed out, the news of his death is etched in memory. Far away in northern Canada, while playing in the front yard, I saw my dad walking toward our house. There was stillness in the air. It was cool and sunny. Deep in thought, my dad had his head hanging low. Always a happy whistling kinda' guy, I knew something was wrong. I felt scared.

"What's wrong daddy?" I hesitantly asked, not wanting to hear the answer. He stopped, looked me square in the eyes and said, "The President died." Leaving me standing there with my mouth open, he kept walking toward the house. "What was a president?" I wondered and "Why did this man's death seem to be such an ominous and tragic event?" Likely taking on my dad's feelings of apparent worry for our future, I also felt stunned. It seemed that life as we knew it would never be the same. An intuitive child, perhaps I sensed that President Kennedy's ideals as expressed in his Inaugural Address, 1961, would continue to be the long delayed something that we all hope for.

Prior to his presidency he received the Purple Heart in 1943 for rescuing fellow sailors in the South Pacific during W.W.II. His popular media attention began with the 'scrubbed and polished look of fine chinaware.' JFK possessed tremendous Irish good looks and women world-wide thought of him as a sexy, sexy beast. The camera loved him. Elected in 1960, it was an era of the Chevrolet, rising skirts, tight sweaters, drive-in theatres and rock 'n roll. It was a time rampant in protests and political idealism.

Considered among the greatest American Presidents, he was a friend to Black African Americans and tried ending racial discrimination. Helping to change the unfairness experienced by Blacks from holding government positions, he appointed about forty Blacks to federal administrative posts. Civil rights activists started taking Freedom Rides, who were supported by JFK. President Kennedy won accolades for being a tough but prudent statesman, earning status as a heraldic icon for a new generation.

His motivation to crack down on organized crime cemented his popularity. He initiated the Peace Corps in the spring of 1961. Making it possible for Americans to volunteer wherever help was needed, President Kennedy became well loved and respected for his political objectives. He believed we could solve our common problems by focusing on similarities, rather than our differences.

The Civil Rights Act of 1964 helped ensure equality and integration without reference to race, color, or creed. By banning racial discrimination in schools, housing and the use of public facilities President Kennedy was a humanitarian in action. Yet despite tinges of emerging social consciousness, many of us continue to think of ourselves as better than and more deserving.

The Space Race was one of the major events to take place during Kennedy's presidency. It inspired many to serve their country (without participating in warfare) by landing the first man on the moon. This goal was achieved in 1969 by American astronaut Neil Armstrong. Still, the Vietnam War permeated its vile. Despite more protests, we continue to war and cling to beliefs such as thinking of ourselves as superior in some way.

The cycle of democracy is built on knowledge …money…power! How is it possible that we live in a world that we did not create, nor often approve of, and at the same time trust that any leader, of any nation, is singularly good enough, or wise enough, to make the decision to war without sharing the stains of blood on our own conscience? I am encouraged by Geneva, Switzerland, having an internet voting system, allowing for the expression of true democracy prior to any decision to war. It is our lack of meaningful democracy and global pursuit to rein superior that will leave in its wake a locusts' destruction and send our souls into everlasting regret.

During W.W.II the world believed in victory through firepower. With America's creation and dropping of the atom bomb on Nagasaki and Hiroshima, killing became impersonal and no longer eye-to-eye in the field. Instead, a lust for political superiority can now blow us all sky-high some night. This current political mode of operandi will be the root cause for plunging us all into everlasting darkness. Our moral maturation lags frighteningly far behind the pace set by science and technology.

The time to admit our wrongs, to forgive and be forgiven has arrived. Because faith without works is dead, now more than ever before there is good reason to be reminded of what we can do for our planet. President John F. Kennedy's eloquent and inspirational messages of hope as expressed in his Inaugural Address can be our mission statement laying the foundation for humankind's need to live as a friend among friends.

Without the aide of a spiritual solution, we will continue to experience the same unhappy outcomes. Wives world-wide will continue to put on their best dress of black voile, holding in their arms only an impersonal flag to keep them warm at night. Occasionally dusting off medals of valor, we will continue to experience unrelenting sorrow and see only our loss. We can step away from those unwilling to participate in the solution. We can step into deep human satisfaction and cease fighting everything and everyone. We can surrender to win.

Our saving grace can be found by committing to the spiritual principle of creating peace within ourselves. Gandhi said: "We have to be the changes we want to see in the world." We can create a different and better outcome for humanity by answering to the call of our evolved moral law within. We must detach from the inner-terrorist that seeks to take us down, keep us down and take us out—permanently. By busting through our illusions and seeing the truth of our own reality, we can change.

Yet we continue to war and suffer for the same underlying reasons—fear and greed. We are afraid of losing what we have and we are afraid of not getting what we want. We are locked into ideas of righteousness and ownership, rather than cooperating in our shared natural resources and responsibilities. By remaining trapped within our fears and need to preserve nationalism at all costs, we continue matriculating in a school for the blind. We continue suffering in isolation with a false sense of security rather than engaging in cooperative ventures.

President John F. Kennedy's assassination on November 22, 1963 was one of the most defining moments in U.S. history, having a traumatic impact on the entire planet and on its political history for ensuing decades. Intended to tarnish his reputation, gossipers slurred that Kennedy was a reckless skirt-chaser. Despite these accusations, he was a doting father to his two young children and an adoring husband to his wife Jacqueline. Murdered in Dallas, Texas, we witnessed the almost infinite expression of desolation in the face of Jacqueline Kennedy (Onassis). Orphaned from their father's love, this one act of gross disrespect for human life caused his family and the lives of people world-wide to feel like bits of a shattered rainbow. Our planet's revered politician died.

We may ask ourselves, have the hearts of people on this planet changed, or do we still long for one who can similarly inspire us all by emphasizing yet again, "With good conscience our only sure reward, with history the final judge of our deeds; let us go forth to lead the land we love, asking [God's] blessing and [God's] help, but knowing that here on earth God's work must truly be our own."

Quick to attach blame, official investigations named Lee Harvey Oswald guilty. However, the allegations of conspiracy surrounding Kennedy's assassination remain a mystery. It is possible the instigating culprit was one of JFK's very own personal henchmen, belonging to his inner circle. His assassination may have been a national cover-up due to the embarrassing fiasco of The Bay of Pigs groupthink decision making process. The decision to overthrow the Cuban government of Fidel Castro, in 1961, was made three months into Kennedy's presidency. Irrespective of who had the most to gain from Kennedy's death, much speculation remains as to what is truth.

There is good and misguided in all of us. That makes us human. We can make things right by owning our part in the bloody outcome of past trespasses. We can change our ways. We can release our penance for justification and embrace new solutions for future conflicts. We can surrender.

Surrendering to love, we step away from temptations to partake in anything we know to be harmful.

When we resolve the battle within, there is no motivation to harm others; we step into humility and we choose life.

Loosing our inclination to judge, we step into avenues of compassionate understanding knowing we are all bits of a rainbow's exquisite design, transforming within at our own time; we trust in the spiritual process and love each other just as we are.

With egos smashed and the "slow implacable fires of human desperation and grass fires extinguished" (Tennessee Williams), we can acknowledge no blade of grass is of greater or lesser importance than the other. We are the sons and daughters of one Creator. If we look for the good we find it. We see the good of our self mirrored in the eyes of others. We can stop repeating the same mistakes based on faulty thinking and beliefs. It is our free choice.

We can alter our future by mending our ways into a fashion different from our forefathers. Together, we can weave into one harmonious fabric of longevity. As long as we have a new day, we can start over again and again until we achieve equality in all societies, peace on earth and goodwill between nations. When we begin to value, honour and respect all life, we need not lay in fields of daisies filled with hearts resting in everlasting regret. We know who we are when we know what we are willing to die for. When will we become willing to take a stand for peace and say, "No more war…No more war?"

Although others may strike out and attack us from their own place of fear and self interest, we can stand firm in our resolve to stay in our own backyard and respond only with non-violence and honest dialogue. We can speak our truth clearly. We will then be taking a stand to die for peace. We can all choose something different. We can throw down the gauntlet and truly begin anew.

Dr. Rita Louise writes, "On September 11, 2001 two planes crashed into the World Trade Center Buildings [the Twin Towers] toppling them to the ground like a house of cards…We are being given a choice. We can choose to be the same or we can choose something different or better. We can take this opportunity to learn to live in harmony with our neighbours, our environment and ourselves. As we rise through the ashes, perhaps it was no mistake that these events occurred on 9-11. Perhaps it was our [unconscious manifestation] of calling God and asking for help."   144

We may call 911, connect and then listen to our moral law within. Since the United Nations purpose is facilitating cooperation, international security, economic development and social equity, it must not be used as a forum for invective. From the grass roots up, together we can guide our elected 191 United Nations member states toward greener pastures. The time to reach meaningful agreement from the global association of governments is now.

Mahatma Gandhi, often referred to as "Great Soul" said that "the most important battle to fight was in overcoming his own demons, fears and insecurities." He is suggesting the importance of making a conscious decision to commit to healing our own anger and resentments, facing and releasing our fears and finding our way to creating our own personal peace. Gandhi is suggesting that this is precisely the courageous inner journey that we are all required to become fully engaged in.

> *When we love ourselves and honour the presence of peace found within our true inner-selves, we will live by the golden rule, effortlessly and willingly: "Thou shalt love thy neighbour as thyself" (Mar 12:31).*
>
> *Again, we are reminded that when we strike out against others, we are energetically striking out against ourselves. We harm our collective unit. We strike God!*

Mahatma Gandhi's view was that "if by strength is meant moral power, then woman is immeasurably man's superior...If nonviolence is the law of our being, the future is with women..." Global peace is enhanced by the growing presence of women in national politics, primarily the Nordic countries. Rwanda, also heading the pack at 48.8% of women parliamentarians, is also a country attempting to rebound following post-war conflicts. With women sharing 50% of the voting power, our time of transit is now.

> *If the hand that rocks the cradle rules the world, will mothers please rise everywhere and, hand in hand with our children, march for peace until our men march with us!*

Knowing we all cry the same, men, such as women, must also become willing to hold and nurture another's child, regardless of race, colour or creed. Because men are beginning to grasp the "we" concept and women are stepping into our own light, truth and power, there is cause for hope. With both parents modeling virtues of self love, equality and respect for life—all life, our children can stop being metaphorically raised with guns in their cribs. We can save our children from fates of becoming future warriors and child suicide bombers. Mother's world-wide can and are leading families and nations by standing firm in our resolve for moral solutions to amoral actions.

Repolishing gems from our past, Gandhi's teachings and President Kennedy's leadership can continue inspiring humanitarians world-wide. Reminding us of the importance of being willing to die without arms for war, we may embrace each other in a spirit of goodwill. Like fine chinaware, the fragility of human relationships and our planet is something we have to take good care of. We have a mutual duty to care, protect and preserve peace by creating harmony amongst humankind.

> *When we make a conscious commitment to create personal peace, planetary peace is already in the making.*
>
> *The universe will support our good decisions in a manner and timing that is magical.*
>
> *Trust this process; it is God working through people.*

Our great reward will be nothing less than harmony with life. When we acknowledge and accept the clarity of loving-kindness that is firmly placed within our beating hearts, we begin co-creating with one good intention.

When we awaken and surrender to love;

* *we become one with God.*

* *we wake up to God consciousness and become enlightened by our love for God and humankind, and*

* *we surrender to one God loving all people, from which is of all life centre and from which we all form a part of its glorious whole.*

> *This priceless gift of awakening to our God consciousness excites within us admiring awe; it is all that is required in valuing every human breath and every living organism on our planet.*
>
> *Reaching our greater destiny will be humankind's course in miracle-making, manifesting an external reality leaving us resting in thankful contemplation for one who exists over and within us all.*

President John F. Kennedy's nobler hopes, beliefs and enduring values for a grand and global alliance assuring a more fruitful life for all can re-root and replant itself within our hearts. The world can consider reigniting his torch of hope and aspiring goals. This torch can be our light, truth and faith in action. Since there is work to be done, we must be willing to make a conscious commitment to join in this beachhead of cooperation and historic effort today. You are my hope. You give me hope for all our children's sake.

Inaugural Address

(in part), January 20, 1961

PRESIDENT JOHN F. KENNEDY
May 29, 1917 – November 22, 1963

[QUOTE] To those old allies whose cultural and spiritual origins we share, we pledge the loyalty of faithful friends. United, there is little we cannot do in a host of cooperative ventures.

To those people in huts and villages across the globe struggling to break the bonds of mass misery, we pledge our best efforts to help them help themselves...If a free society cannot help the many who are poor, it cannot save the few who are rich...to convert our good words into good deeds.

To that world assembly of sovereign states, the United Nations, our last best hope in an age where the instruments of war have far outpaced the instruments of peace, we renew our pledge of support—to prevent it from becoming merely a forum for invective—to strengthen its shield of the new and the weak—and to enlarge the area in which its writ may run.

Finally, to those nations who would make themselves our adversary, we offer not a pledge but a request: that both sides begin anew the quest for peace, before the dark powers of destruction unleashed by science engulf all humanity in planned or accidental self-destruction...Let us never negotiate out of fear.

And if a beachhead of cooperation may push back the jungle of suspicion, let both sides join in creating a new endeavor, not a new balance of power, but a new world of law, where the strong are just and the weak secure and the peace preserved.

The graves of young Americans who answered the call to service around the globe...Now the trumpet summons us again—not as a call to bear arms, though arms we need; not as a call to battle, though embattled we are—but a call to bear the burden of a long twilight struggle, year in and year out, "rejoicing in hope, patient in tribulation"—a struggle against the common enemies of man: tyranny, poverty, disease and war itself.

Can we forge against these enemies a grand and global alliance, North and South, East and West, that can assure a more fruitful life for all Humankind? Will you join in that historic effort?

In the long history of the world, only a few generations have been granted the role of defending freedom in its hour of maximum danger. I do not shrink from this responsibility—I welcome it. I do not believe that any of us would exchange places with any other people or any other generation. The energy, the faith, the devotion which we bring to this endeavour will light our country and all who serve it—and the glow from that fire can truly light the world.

And so, my fellow Americans: ask not what your country can do for you—ask what you can do for your country.

My fellow citizens of the world: ask not what America will do for you, but what together we can do for the freedom of man.

With a good conscience our only sure reward, with history the final judge of our deeds, let us go forth to lead the land we love, asking His blessing and His help, but knowing that here on earth God's work must truly be our own [END QUOTE].

We are responsible for mastery against the common enemies of man: anger, fear, pride and righteousness itself. Knowing that united there is little we cannot do for the benefit of all we may ask and sense what comes, "What can we do for the freedom of man? What are the most loving, kind and respectful things we can do for life today?" As we continue to chart the course of human history, we may remember the charred remains of firestorms past and vow to war no more. When we abandon ourselves to infinite resources of protection and care, we may begin to free ourselves from ourselves: Let us love one another and allow for life to renew itself.

A Call for Unity

Mine is a voice calling from the wilderness,
where stillness reigns, long since forgotten,
"Can anyone hear? Is anyone there? Does anyone care?"

If you cannot hear, listen.
If you are not there, be present.
If you do not care, care.
Hear this calling.

Mine is a heart promising to hold your heart in mine,
as you hold my heart in yours.
We are beating hearts, becoming one pulse for life.
One Heart

Mine is a mind holding your thoughts in mine,
as you hold my thoughts in yours.
We are many thoughts, becoming one good intention.
One Mind

Mine is a spirit freely sharing your breath with mine.
Breathe deeply and completely.
We are many breaths, becoming one mystical flow.
One Spirit

Mine is an energy lighting your sphere,
as you light my own.
We are rays of light, becoming one exquisite glow.
One Light

We are remembering to live in harmony
with self, nature and nations.
Aligning
Integrating
Balancing
We are becoming one people on one planet.
One Family

We are awakening to our
One Heart
One Mind
One Spirit
One Light
One Family
We are becoming whole.

Mine is a voice calling from the wilderness,
where stillness reigns, and you came.
Lighter and freer,
we are loving-kindness in calming balm.
We are peace on earth, goodwill toward humankind.
~Randi Dong

Summary Points

Open for group discussion, or suggested essay topics.

1. It's a spiritual life.
2. We care about life — all life.
3. God is God is God, and by any other name God is still God.

4. As we polish our true self, our God self, we begin to shine and live in partnership with God; we become part of God's glorious journey of creation.

5. Are we God's Barbie dolls busily creating atom bombs, robots without moral thinking-checks and other such genetic Frankenstein mutations? Or, are we fleshy and energetic thinking souls empowered by God's calling for life enhancing free choices?

6. We know that when we strike out against another, we are energetically striking out against ourselves and harming our collective unit. We strike God!

7. Life is manifest as belief personified. If our external reality is a reflection of our inner reality and we don't like what we see exterior to us, we must change within. We can know peace and live peace.

8. "Am I God's dolly?" At birth we have knowingness that we are all the sons and daughters of one God. But this sense of oneness is often kyboshed due to our inability to reconcile the bad things that happen in life with belief systems that preach about a loving and merciful God.

9. We start to realize that God works through people who are willing to help and to be helped. We begin to trust in life.

10. Part of a healing journey of spiritual renewal is to connect with a loving Creator and to begin to remember and reclaim our true self; it is our innocence and love for life – all life.

11. When I would ask, "What do you think I should do...advise me?" Mom always said the same, "Randi, I cannot live your life for you. You have to live your own life."

12. Surrendering to love, we grow closer to our former knowingness of oneness with an all encompassing, all pervasive truth—God is love. We not only begin living with God in our hearts, we begin living within the heart of God.

13. If you are suffering, I can assure you there is cause for hope. There is light at the end of the tunnel and this light exists in the centre of us all. This light is love; it is life itself.

14. As God's creations, we remember spirit and reconnect with our creator within. When we do, we have no cause to harm others; we end war and unite in an intention to create world peace and harmony with life—all life.

15. The presence of God's compassion and kindness is found in our ability to bring comfort and care to each other. God works through people willing to be a channel of helpfulness, love and goodwill. When we look for the good, we find it; we grow, become grateful for all and accepting of what is. We trust in God.

16. "God does not play dice with our lives" (Albert Einstein). When we surrender to love, we return to peace of mind, divine and loving universal mind. We trust the cards we are dealt are perfectly placed for purposes promising our greatest benefit.

17. By remaining trapped within self-centered perceptions of grandiosity, we blindly remain in a stage that has no alternative but to perpetuate the same outcomes. War. All such life negating beliefs and actions must be eradicated or we shall surely become "like bits of a shattered rainbow."

18. JFK possessed tremendous Irish good looks and women world-wide thought of him as a sexy, sexy beast. The camera loved him. "What is a President?"

19. Because men are beginning to grasp the "we" concept and women are stepping into our own light, truth and power, there is cause for hope. With both parents modeling virtues of self love, equality and respect for life—all life, our children can stop being metaphorically raised with guns in their cribs. We can save our children from fates of becoming future warriors and child suicide bombers.

20. Mother's world-wide can and are leading families and nations by standing firm in our resolve for moral solutions to amoral actions.

21. When we surrender to love, we become one with God. Awakening to God consciousness, we are enlightened by love for self, God and humankind. We surrender to one God loving all people, from which is of all life centre and from which we all form a part of its glorious whole.

22. This priceless gift of awakening to God consciousness excites within us admiring awe; it is all that is required in valuing every human breath and every living organism on our planet.

23. Reaching our greater destiny will be humankind's course in miracle-making, manifesting an external reality leaving us resting in thankful contemplation for one who exists over and within us all.

> *Resting*
> *in thankful*
> *contemplation*
> *we see clearly,*
> *Truth...Beauty...Love,*
> *raising within us a shining*
> *alighting our eternal All; we are one.* 161

WORKS CITED

DONNE, JOHN   MANKINDE

EINSTEIN, ALBERT   Quotes:
                         http://www.thinkexist.com/english/Author/x/A
                         uthor_1082_1html

GANDHI, MAHATMA   (Int.1)
                         http://en.wikipedia.org/wiki/Mahatma_Gandhi
                         #Assassination

THE GREAT QUOTATIONS   Compiled by George Seldes. Pocket Books, a
                         division of Simon and Schuster, Inc., New
                         York, N.Y. This Pocket Book edition is
                         published by arrangement with Lyle Stuart,
                         Inc., and Irving Caesar. 1967.

KENNEDY, PRESIDENT JOHN F., INAUGURAL ADDRESS (in part)
January 20, 1961   (http://www.bartleby.com/124/press56.html)
                         F. Kennedy, US President, Quote:
                         http://www.bellaonline.com/articles/art6453.asp

K.J.V. THE HOLY BIBLE CONCORDANCE,
                         "Genesis." Memorial Bibles International, Inc.
                         1974.

LOUISE, DR. RITA   http://www.soulhealer.com/ashes.html

POPE, ALEXANDER   An Essay on Man, Epistle I, 1733

SHAKESPEARE, WILLIAM   Julius Caesar (III, i, 86 and II, ii, 69) Hamlet (I, iii)

WILLIAMS, TENNESSEE   "The Glass Menagerie" (pp 1177-1222),
                         Angles of Vision, Reading, Writing, and the
                         Study of Literature, by Arthur W. Biddle
                         and Toby Fulwiler. McGraw-Hill, Inc. 1992.

DISCLAIMER: The sources of philosophic quotes used in A Philosopher's Dilemma
               are from various internet websites and not from original publications;
               they have not been verified for accuracy.

About the Author

1956—

Fort St. James,
British Columbia,
Canada

Randi Done

*"Yet howsoever changed or tossed, not even a wreath of mist is lost.
No atom shall itself exhaust. So shall the soul live on and
run its endless course in God's unlimited universe."*

Born to emigrant parents from Norway, I was raised on a cattle ranch near a remote logging community in north-central British Columbia. Besides writing, I love tromping through the forest on old game trails, to be married, a mom and student of life.

If by sharing what has felt so freely gifted to me this book has been helpful in uplifting one human spirit beyond the realm of self and into a sphere of wholeness, I am thankful.

Reaching Our Greater Destiny was written near the beach in Peachland, Canada (2006-2007)

The five winning entries contributed to the
Clem Battye Poetry Competition—2007
and included in this book are;

Our Glory Whole, Better than Gold,
Awakening, Thankful and
A Call for Unity

Judges comments;

Hope reads between the lines!
Very deep thought process.
Calming—Uplifting—
Very impressive!
"Awakening"
is brilliant!

Outstanding Literary Achievement

The Editors of the International Library of Poetry were 'thrilled' to inform the author, Randi Done, that "Awakening" was honored with the prestigious 2007 Editor's Choice Award for outstanding literary achievement. To further commemorate this achievement Randi Done received the Editor's Choice Commemorative Bronze Medallion and the Editor's Published Poet Ribbon Award Pin for her "artistic accomplishments and unique perspective—characteristics found in the most noteworthy poetic works" (2007).

167

Panorama Publishing Co.

Box 1127, Peachland, British Columbia, V0H 1X0, CANADA
email randi@panorama-publishing.ca

Unity Verses

An Original Series of Inspirational Prints
CREATED JUST FOR YOU

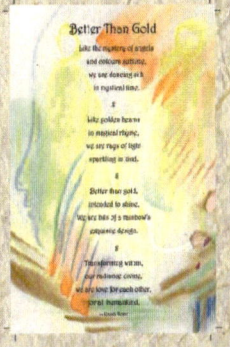

REACHING

OUR GLORY WHOLE

BETTER THAN GOLD

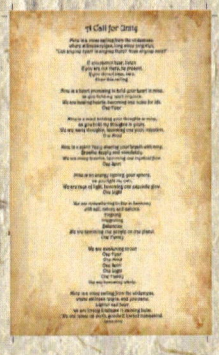

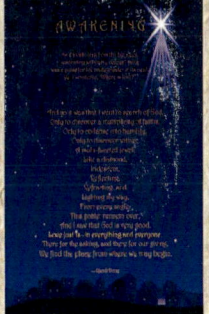

RESTING

A CALL FOR UNITY

AWAKENING

IT MATTERS

To view all products and prices, please visit our internet website @

www.panorama-publishing.ca

THANK YOU FOR SHOPPING WITH PANORAMA PUBLISHING CO.

Smile;

extend a helping hand,

a kind word and remember,

love is the bond that binds us all.

God loves us best through each other.